Pestle and mortar

Paintbrushes
made from
animal hair

Eyewitness
LEONARDO
DA VINCI

Written by
ANDREW LANGLEY

Renaissance hunting horn

Ornate 16th-century keys

Ivory jester's sticks

Cameo pendant

Giambologna's *Rape of the Sabine Women,* carved from a single block of stone

DK

LONDON, NEW YORK,
MELBOURNE, MUNICH, and DELHI

Project editor Carey Scott
Art editor Cheryl Telfer
Senior managing editor Linda Martin
Senior managing art editor Julia Harris
Production Kate Oliver
Picture research Sean Hunter
DTP Designer Andrew O'Brien
Consultant David Herman
Photographer Andy Crawford
Researcher Charlotte Beauchamp

PAPERBACK EDITION
Managing editor Camilla Hallinan
Managing art editor Sophia M Tampakopoulos
Senior editor Fran Jones
Senior art editor Owen Peyton-Jones
Editor and reference compiler Sue Nicholson
Art editor Andrew Nash
Production Luca Bazzoli
Picture research Jo Walton & Julia Harris-Voss
DTP designer Siu Yin Chan
Cover designer Emy Manby

16th-century mirror with convex glass

This Eyewitness ® Guide has been conceived by
Dorling Kindersley Limited and Editions Gallimard

Hardback edition first published in Great Britain in 1999
This edition published in Great Britain in 2006
by Dorling Kindersley Limited,
80 Strand, London WC2R 0RL

Colour reproduction by
Colourscan, Singapore
Printed and bound in China by Toppan

Discover more at
www.dk.com

Contents

Woolworkers' Guild emblem

The early Renaissance

LEONARDO DA VINCI was born near Florence, Italy, in 1452. The period known as the Middle Ages, which had endured since the fall of the Roman Empire, was gradually drawing to a close and a new age was beginning. Leonardo's Italy was at the centre of a period of intense creativity, which we now call the Renaissance, meaning "rebirth". There was a revival of interest in the classical works of Greece and Rome, which inspired a new way of looking at the world. Thinkers turned away from the medieval preoccupation with saving souls and avoiding temptation, and began instead to explore people's individuality, and to educate them in their duties to society. This became a movement known as humanism. At the same time, artists celebrated the beauty of the human body in more lifelike paintings and sculptures.

SCRIPT SCRAPER
The scribe held a quill or stylus in his right hand and a scraper tool like this in his left. He used it to scratch out any mistakes and to sharpen the tip of his quill. All the same, many errors were made in the copying, which were then repeated, sometimes leading to major inaccuracies.

Handle to hold parchment flat

Lamp containing fat and wick

Nearly all texts were written in Latin

Parchment for cleaning ink spills

MONASTIC MONOPOLY
During the Middle Ages, books were scarce and precious. Each one was copied out by hand by a professional scribe or a monk. At sloping desks in the monastery's "scriptorium", the monks painstakingly produced manuscripts of religious texts, beautifully decorated, or illuminated, with coloured inks. Much schooling also took place in monasteries, convents, and cathedrals. This concentration of texts and education gave the Catholic Church a great deal of power, and reinforced its position at the centre of medieval life in Europe.

Inkwell and stylus

ART OR CRAFT?
Artists in the early 15th century were regarded simply as craftsmen. Sculptors, like the one shown chiselling a figure on this relief, would have been members of a crafts union, called the Stonemason's Guild.

Stonemason measures proportions

Slits through which arrows were shot

DECLINE OF THE CASTLE
The thick walls of Caerphilly Castle, Wales, stand stark and forbidding. More than 12,000 medieval castles were built in Britain and France alone. They were massive strongholds designed as fortifiedbases for soldiers. In the mid-15th century, the development of firearms and explosives powerful enough to destroy the strongest walls spelt the end of the castle's dominance.

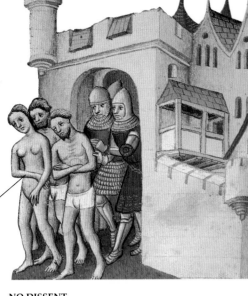

Cathars being expelled from the city of Carcassone in France

NO DISSENT
The Catholic Church of the Middle Ages was intolerant of anyone who contradicted its beliefs. People who belonged to extreme sects, like these Cathars, were often tortured, killed, or exiled. After the 1400s, humanist thinkers tried to encourage a more tolerant attitude.

A fanciful portrait of 1553 shows Genghis Khan dressed as a Western ruler

CORRIDOR TO THE EAST
Mongol armies from the Asian Steppes, inspired by the great conqueror Genghis Khan, built up a vast empire in the early 13th century. In 1241, the Mongols devastated Hungary and threatened Western Europe. Yet their conquests also made it possible for European traders, including Marco Polo, to visit the Far East, thereby stimulating trade and encouraging explorers to find easier sea routes to the East.

...AM'S ADVANCE
...r nearly 1,000 years, Constantinople ...s the capital of Christianity's Eastern ...yzantine) Empire. But in 1453, the Ottoman ...rks besieged and captured the city, which ...came a major capital of the Islamic world. ...is event, shown above, brought one great ...ofit to the West – the arrival of refugee ...olars, who possessed valuable insights ...o classical Greek language and literature.

Discovering the past

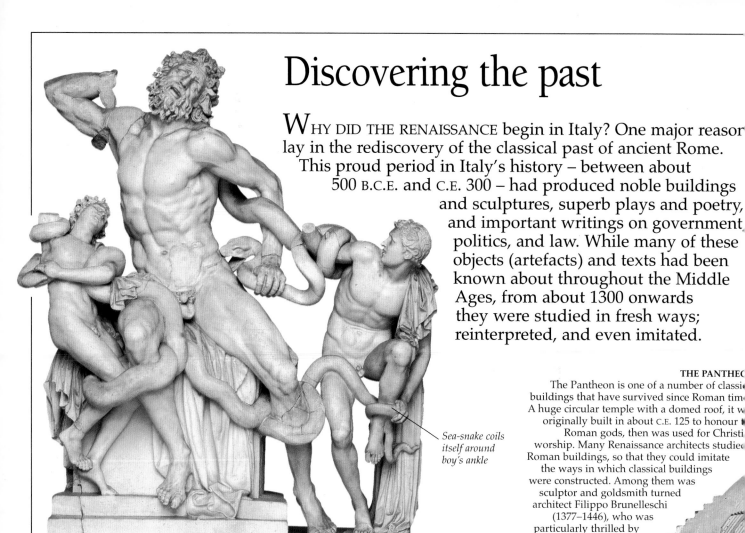

WHY DID THE RENAISSANCE begin in Italy? One major reason lay in the rediscovery of the classical past of ancient Rome. This proud period in Italy's history – between about 500 B.C.E. and C.E. 300 – had produced noble buildings and sculptures, superb plays and poetry, and important writings on government, politics, and law. While many of these objects (artefacts) and texts had been known about throughout the Middle Ages, from about 1300 onwards they were studied in fresh ways; reinterpreted, and even imitated.

Sea-snake coils itself around boy's ankle

THE PANTHEON

The Pantheon is one of a number of classical buildings that have survived since Roman times. A huge circular temple with a domed roof, it was originally built in about C.E. 125 to honour the Roman gods, then was used for Christian worship. Many Renaissance architects studied Roman buildings, so that they could imitate the ways in which classical buildings were constructed. Among them was sculptor and goldsmith turned architect Filippo Brunelleschi (1377–1446), who was particularly thrilled by the Pantheon.

Rectangular portico supported by eight pillars

EPIC INSPIRATION

In 1506, an ancient Greek sculpture known as the *Laocoon* was unearthed near Rome. It was brought to the Vatican by Pope Julius II (1443–1513), one of the great patrons of the Renaissance. Carved in about 30 B.C.E., it shows a scene from the story of Troy. The priest Laocoon and his sons are crushed by two giant sea-snakes, an incident described by the Roman poet Virgil in his epic story *The Aeneid*. This sculpture, with its dramatic representation of emotion, deeply impressed many Italian artists and sculptors, notably Michelangelo (1475–1564).

ANCIENT MASTERS

This frontispiece to Servius' *Commentary on Virgil* was painted by Simone Martini in about 1340. The book belonged to the Italian poet Petrarch (1304–74), who made many neglected Latin texts available, compiled biographies of famous Romans, and even wrote a letter to the long-dead philosopher Cicero.

Latin text

GRACES FROM GREECE
This sculpture, called *The Three Graces*, dates from Greece's Hellenistic period (323–30 B.C.E.), and depicts three attendants to the goddess Venus. For Italian scholars, the world of ancient Greece was far more remote than that of ancient Rome. However, after the fall of Byzantium in 1453, many Greek scholars took refuge in Italy. Interest in Greek culture grew rapidly, and the Graces became familiar figures in the sculpture and painting of Renaissance Italy.

GRACES FROM FLORENCE
Sandro Botticelli (1445–1510) clearly based the Graces in his painting *Primavera* (Spring), on classical models. The grouping and posture are clear echoes of the original sculpture. Botticelli's Graces also conform with the ancient Roman author Seneca's description of the goddesses as "clad in loosened transparent gowns". The choice of subject reflects the Renaissance fascination with both Greek myths and sculpture.

Loose, transparent gowns, as described by Seneca

Oculus (opening) at the top lights the interior

Span of the dome is an amazing 43 m (142 ft)

Columns supporting the porch and entrance arch

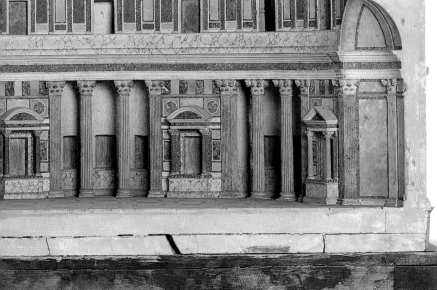

CIRCLE IN A SQUARE
Brunelleschi used classical Roman ideas about proportion and technique in his own projects. His design for the Pazzi Chapel in Florence incorporated the harmony of form he had noted in the Pantheon, based on a circle placed within a square. Work on this small, but perfectly balanced, building began in about 1430.

THE PLATONIC ACADEMY
Perhaps the most important of the rediscovered Greek authors was the philosopher Plato. His theories had a huge impact on Renaissance thinking. Plato's ideas, and those of his teacher Socrates, were eagerly discussed by the members of an informal assembly called the Academy. They met near Florence at the villa of the influential Medici family.

City-states of Italy

WHEN LEONARDO WAS BORN, Italy was not a single country. Much of it was split up into small city-states that ruled themselves. As their prosperity grew, the city-states developed their own forms of self-government. Some, such as Florence, were republics where the citizens elected their own leaders and councils. Others, such as Milan, were duchies controlled by a single unelected family. Northern Italy had the biggest and most prosperous cities in Europe. Two growing classes – the craftworkers and merchants – made up most of the population of the cities. The craftworkers produced a large variety of goods, which the merchants then sold all over Europe.

TRAINING A GENIUS
This document records Leonardo's admission into the Florentine artists' guild at the age of 20. From 1469, Leonardo trained in the workshop of celebrated painter, sculptor, and goldsmith Andrea del Verrocchio (1435–88).

Decoration in enamelling and gilt

Latin motto means "Love requires Faith"

VENETIAN GLASS
Venice was famous for its wonderful glassware. This goblet was produced in Murano, the centre of the Venetian glass industry. The goblet was a betrothal gift between two powerful families. The betrothed pair are portrayed, one on either side of the glass.

SUMPTUOUS CERAMICS
The first majolica (pottery decorated in bright colours over a glazed white background) was imported into Italy from Spain in about 1450. The style became so popular that workshops for producing majolica sprang up all over the country. The most notable majolica craftsmen worked in the city of Urbino, which, despite its small size, had become an important cultural centre. This plate was part of an ornate dinner service commissioned by a wealthy family.

Story of the ancient Greek gods Apollo and Pan is depicted on the plate

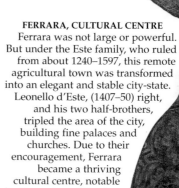

MILAN, CITY OF THE SFORZAS
Under the rule of the Visconti family, Milan had been the most powerful and ambitious of Italy's city-states, and Florence's most dangerous enemy. But in 1450, the dukedom passed to Francesco Sforza (1401–66), right, a mercenary soldier who became a strong and peace-loving prince. Francesco's second son, Lodovico (1451–1508), was one of the most powerful figures of Renaissance Italy. He was also a generous patron of the arts, and employed Leonardo for 18 years.

FERRARA, CULTURAL CENTRE
Ferrara was not large or powerful. But under the Este family, who ruled from about 1240–1597, this remote agricultural town was transformed into an elegant and stable city-state. Leonello d'Este, (1407–50) right, and his two half-brothers, tripled the area of the city, building fine palaces and churches. Due to their encouragement, Ferrara became a thriving cultural centre, notable for its music and theatre.

CRAFTSMEN CITIZENS
All citizens of Florence could vote or stand for office. But to be a citizen one had to be accepted by a guild – one of the trade associations representing the 21 useful professions, or trades. Each guild had its own emblem, such as that of the woolworkers, shown here.

[IR]ON MEN
[Mil]anese smiths [pro]duced some of the finest [me]talwork in Europe, from [ma]gnificent suits of armour [to] delicate keys and locks.

ITALY IN ABOUT 1490
The major independent city-states were grouped in the northern half of the peninsula, which had more fertile farmland and better trade links with the rest of Europe. In the centre were the Papal States, ruled from Rome. Most of southern Italy was the separate kingdom of Naples, which was to fall into the hands of Spain in 1504.

URBINO, CITY OF LEARNING
Federico da Montefeltro (1422–82), Duke of Urbino, lost his right eye and part of his nose in a tournament, and so was always portrayed from the left. Though he was an outstanding soldier who served both the papacy and Lorenzo de' Medici as a *condottiere* (mercenary soldier), the duke is remembered as a humane and learned ruler, and a patron of the arts. He deplored the printing of books, and assembled one of the biggest libraries of handwritten manuscripts in Europe.

FLORENCE THE REPUBLIC
The wealthy banking family of the Medici dominated Florence from the mid-15th century. Lorenzo de' Medici (1449–92) was determined to extend the family's power base. While his first son was destined to inherit his position in Florence, his second son Giovanni (1475–1521) was trained in the Church from the age of eight. Thanks to family influence, he eventually rose to become pope in 1513, adopting the name of Leo X.

13

Renaissance men

I N 1860 JACOB BURCKHARDT, an historian of the Renaissance, referred to Leonardo as the "universal man". Leonardo, he argued, had excelled in every branch of study, from painting and sculpture to botany and mathematics. Today he seems the essential example of a Renaissance man – an all-rounder whose talents combined the arts and sciences. But the term means more than this. To a European of the 16th century, the "universal man" was not just a scholar and artist, but also a fine swordsman and horseman, a witty talker, a graceful orator, a skilled musician, and a responsible citizen.

King Henry is pictured dressed in the height of Renaissance finery

EVERY INCH A KI
As a young man, He
VIII of England
everything. Tall
handsome, he co
ride all day, win jou
speak four langua
play the lute, and
learnedly about relig
and astrono

PASSIONATE GENIUS
Michelangelo was one of the most astonishing figures of the Renaissance. He designed tombs, fortifications, and cathedral domes. His sculpture of David was hugely influential. But his masterpiece was the painting of biblical scenes on the ceiling of the Sistine Chapel in Rome.

Silk hose and garter

Michelangelo
(1475–1564)

King Henry VIII
(1491–1547)

Equestrian portraits were popular during the Renaissance

PRINCE AND PATRON
François I of France (1494–1547)
ell in love with Renaissance Italy.
He collected paintings and
sculptures and built eight grand
new castles, sumptuously
decorated by Italian craftsmen.
He even invited the ageing
Leonardo to live in France.

Arms reaching upwards form a circle

PERFECT PROPORTIONS
The vast range of Leonardo's
interests included geometry. He used
the theories of the Roman architect
Vitruvius to show how the arms and
legs of a human figure could describe
both a perfect square and a perfect
circle. These two shapes, he believed,
formed the basis of everything else in
the universe.

Figure standing upright forms a square

*irer completed
00 drawings,
0 woodcuts,
d more than
0 engravings*

MASTER OF ART
The German painter and engraver
Albrecht Dürer was the greatest artist of
the Renaissance in northern Europe. He
mastered every aspect of graphic art,
from oil and watercolour painting to
etching and woodcutting. He also
pioneered engraving techniques,
which allowed his work to be
reproduced easily and
taken all over the
continent.

Ancient Greek robe

RESTLESS MIND
The Italian painter
Raphael (1483–1520)
depicted Leonardo as
the Greek philosopher
Plato. This was ironic,
for Leonardo never
learned to read Greek
or Latin, despite many
attempts. Yet in almost
every other field of
study he was dazzlingly
gifted. "Everywhere, his
mind turned to difficult
matters," wrote his
biographer, Giorgio
Vasari. Having mastered
painting, Leonardo
turned to anatomy,
bridge-building, the
design of war machines,
architecture, mathematics,
natural history, geology,
and philosophy. He also
wrote fables and drew maps.

Albrecht Dürer
(1471–1528)

Leonardo
da Vinci
(1452–1519)

The new trade

MEDICI EMBLEM
The six balls on the Medici family insignia may represent coins to show that they were bankers.

By 1460, ITALIAN MERCHANTS were able to offer a wider variety of goods than ever before. There were spices from the Far East, iron and tin from England, leatherwork from Spain, cotton and gold thread from the Levant (Eastern Mediterranean), and woollen cloth from Florence. The demand for such exotic products had grown swiftly during the century as towns became wealthier and society more stable. Traders ventured ever further in their search for new supplies. From the 1420s, Portuguese sailors pushed steadily down the West African coast until, in 1498, Vasco da Gama rounded the Cape of Good Hope and reached India. Five years earlier, a Spanish expedition led by the explorer Christopher Columbus had crossed the Atlantic and reached the "New World" of America.

Chine
si

VALIANT VENTURER
Jacques Coeur (1395–1456) was a highly successful French merchant and banker. He became chancellor to King Charles VII and took charge of royal finances. Made a nobleman in 1448, he adopted the motto "To the valiant heart nothing is impossible".

Gap where America ought to be

West African coast

EMPTY OCEAN
The Portuguese reached the Far East by sailing eastwards. Columbus set out in 1492 believing that he would reach Japan by travelling west. World maps of the time, such as this globe, showed nothing in the "Western Ocean" between Africa and Asia. The existence of the American continent was unknown in Europe. When Columbus landed in the Bahamas, he was still convinced he was near the East Indies, and searched in vain for gold and spices.

Fugger became known as "Jakob the Rich"

ROYAL BANKERS
The German Jakob Fugger (1459–1525) founded one of the earliest banking firm in Europe. In 1491, the Fugger bank le the Duke of Tyrol (who later became the Emperor Maximilian I) 200,000 florins to finance a war. In return the duke gave the Fuggers exclusive right to copper and silver mines, which the modernized and made profitable. Li some other businessmen of the tim Fugger employed a fortune-tel to predict the resu of his deals.

SILK MILLS
Although luxury goods continued to be imported from the Far East, merchants wanted to produce exotic goods, such as silk cloth, within Europe. Lucca was the first silk-weaving centre in Italy, but by 1500 Florence had replaced Lucca as the leader. The mechanical silk-twisting mills of Florence became famous for their fine brocades and velvets.

Cloves

Fine
Italian silks

*Damask
(woven
design)*

Peppercorns

Cinnamon

ADDED SPICE
Spices had been a great luxury since the Middle Ages. But when Portuguese sailors began to trade directly with India and the Far East, spices became much more widely available in Europe.

OINS OF ITALY
e main city-states of
ly each had their own
rrencies. But by 1450,
e florin had become
e most important
rrency in all of
rope. This small
ld coin – no
gger than a
gernail – was
amped with a
y, emblem of the
y of Florence.

Coins
from
Rome

SALESMAN'S KIT
Travelling merchants carried their goods or samples in a bag such as this. Around the outside of the bag are small pockets in which sealed bags of coins were kept. Florins were made of valuable 24-carat gold, and were a favourite target of coin clippers, who illegally shaved gold from the edges for their own use.

Florins

Pocket for coins

Memorial fresco by the Florentine painter Paolo Uccello (1397–1475)

IOANNES·ACVTVS·EQVES·BRITANNICVS·DVCAETATIS·S VAE·CAVTISSIMVS·E·TREI·MILITARIS·PERITISSIMVS·HABITVS·EST

Governing the people

Tʜʀᴏᴜɢʜᴏᴜᴛ ᴛʜᴇ ᴍɪᴅᴅʟᴇ ᴀɢᴇs, most of Europe consisted of small states that constantly fought with one another. But strong rulers, helped by growing economic prosperity, gradually welded these states together into larger units. By the beginning of the 16th century, the first nation-states had emerged. Among them were France and England, whose parliaments of noblemen passed laws and gathered taxes. Much of Italy, on the other hand, was split between two old rivals – the pope and the emperor. The pope controlled central Italy, while the emperor ruled the Holy Roman Empire (Germany and northern Italy). Both were elected rulers. The self-governing city-states, such as Florence, soon found it hard to keep their independence.

SOLDIER FOR HIRE
Although born in England, Sir John Hawkwood (c. 1320–94) served in Italy as a *condottiere*, or mercenary soldier. Many city-states employed bands of mercenary troops to protect them or attack their rivals. This left the city's craftsmen and businessmen free to carry on their work during times of war.

A KING'S DIVINE RIGHT
The English King Henry VIII presides over the House of Lords, one of England's two houses of Parliament, in 1523. The bishops sit on the left, the judges in the centre, and the noblemen on the right. In England, as in many northern countries, the king's authority was believed to be God-given. However, Henry's decisions had to be approved by his Parliament, and he relied on it to grant him money.

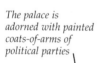

The palace is adorned with painted coats-of-arms of political parties

Bell tower

PALACE OF POWER
The Palazzo Vecchio (Old Palace) was the centre of government in Florence, where the elected councils sat. Completed in about 1310, it boasted the city's tallest tower, from which hung a huge bell to warn the citizens in times of danger, or to summon them for public meetings. The Medici family moved here in 1540, and both Leonardo and Michelangelo were commissiond to produce paintings for the interior.

PRACTICAL POLITICS
The sarcastic smile of politician and writer Niccolo Machiavelli (1469–1527) reveals his low opinion of human nature. Not surprisingly, his view of politics was gloomy but straightforward: the end justifies the means. His book *The Prince* advised rulers to be as ruthless and deceitful as necessary to bring order and peace to the lives of their corrupt subjects. "It is much safer for a prince to be feared than loved," he wrote.

Portrait of Machiavelli by ...nti di Tito

Savonarola's execution on the Piazza della Signoria by an unknown artist

THE PERFECT STATE
This woodcut is from a book called *Utopia*, written in 1516 by the English statesman Sir Thomas More (1478–1535). *Utopia* describes an ideal society on an island in the New World (America). In this Utopia (the Greek for "nowhere"), all people are equal, all possessions are shared, and all religions are tolerated. More was a deeply religious man who refused to compromise his principles. But English society was not as tolerant as that in the imaginary Utopia, and More was eventually executed for refusing to recognize Henry VIII as head of the English church.

Boat carrying explorers to Utopia

DEATH OF A DOOM MONGER
By the 1490s, Florence's great age was over. The fiery preacher Girolamo Savonarola (1452–98) denounced the greed and corruption of its citizens, and prophesied invasion from the north as punishment. In 1494, Charles VIII of France indeed marched into the city. Briefly, Savonarola was the most powerful figure in Florence, but in 1498 he was found guilty of heresy and was hanged and burned.

PRIDE OF LIONS
The Florentines took the lion as their heraldic symbol. From the 13th century, real lions were kept caged in the city centre. They were finally removed in the 18th century when people complained of the smell! Stone lions guard the entrance to the Palazzo Vecchio. They flank a Latin inscription that once claimed Jesus Christ as the elected king of Florence, implying that no mortal ruler could have absolute power. The inscription was altered in 1851.

Later inscription means "King of Kings, Lord of Lords"

Stone lion is a symbol of the Florentine republic

City of the Medici

The Medusa's gaze was said to turn people to stone

In about 1466, the young Leonardo moved with his family from Vinci to Florence. The city he entered was vibrant and prosperous. Most of its finest buildings were already completed, but many of the greatest masters of the Italian Renaissance were still at work there. The Medici, a wealthy banking family, were a hugely powerful influence in the city. The modest Cosimo the Elder (1389–1464) was succeeded, briefly, by his son Piero (1416–69), and then by h flamboyant grandson Lorenzo the Magnificent. The Medici not only directed the city's government and policies, but also spent vast sums in commissioning paintings, sculpture and architectural designs from the finest artists available.

ENEMIES BEWARE
Duke Cosimo de' Medici commissioned Benvenuto Cellini (1500–71) to create this triumphant bronze statue of Perseus in 1545. It shows the mythical hero holding aloft the severed head of the evil Medusa – intended as a warning to Cosimo's enemies. During the casting, Cellini ran out of bronze and had to melt down his own pewter plates and bowls.

Headless body of the Medusa

VIEW OF A CITY
This is the Florence that Leonardo woul have seen as a youn man. The painting is based on a woodcut made in about 1470. The River Arno runs through the middle of the city, and medieval walls surround it.

Florence's great cathedral dome

THE MARZOCCO
The lion was the symbol of Florentine power. Statues were set up in towns ruled by the city, and prisoners were once made to kiss the lion's backside. This very human-looking lion, called the *Marzocco*, was carved by Donatello (1386–1466) in 1420, and originally sported a gilded crown.

Shield bearing a lily, the city's emblem

GRAND DUKE COSIMO
Though Florence freed itself briefly from the Medici twice during the Wars of Italy (1494–1512 and 1527–30), the family continued to govern the city's affairs. Cosimo I (1519–74), known as Cosimo the Great, was one of the most successful family members; he became Grand Duke of Tuscany in 1569.

DEADLY RIVALS
The Medici had many enemies in Florence, including the wealthy Pazzi family, whose emblem showed a pair of dolphins. In 1478, the Pazzi tried to seize powe by attacking Lorenzo as h prayed in the cathedral an murdering his brother Giuliano. But the coup failed and the assassins were execute

MAGNIFICO
~~Lo~~renzo de' Medici has become known ~~as~~ "the Magnificent". He was not only ~~a~~ charming leader and generous ~~pa~~tron but also a skilful athlete ~~(es~~pecially at football) and huntsman, ~~a~~ fine poet, and a practical joker.

~~A~~DORING FAMILY
~~In~~ about 1475, a friend of Piero de' Medici ~~co~~mmissioned Sandro Botticelli to paint the ~~Ad~~oration of the Magi. This was a conventional ~~su~~bject for the time, showing the Wise Men ~~w~~orshipping the infant Jesus and the Virgin ~~M~~ary. But as an exercise in flattery, Botticelli ~~pl~~aced portraits of prominent members of the ~~M~~edici family in his painting – as ~~w~~ell as a self-portrait!

FINE BINDINGS
Cosimo the Elder and his heirs built up the massive Medici Library, which contained over 10,000 classical and medieval texts. When the Medici were exiled in 1494, the library was seized by the city council and placed here in the cloisters of the convent of San Marco, which became Europe's first public library.

Arcaded courtyard inside the palace

COSIMO'S PALACE
The Medici Palace, begun in the 1440s, was a grand and imposing building. But Cosimo the Elder found it far from cozy. "Too large a house for so small a family", he said, after the death of his second son. He preferred to relax amid the olive groves of his country villas.

Lorenzo as a young man

Giuliano, Piero's son

Cosimo the Elder is shown kneeling before the baby Jesus

Piero, Cosimo the Elder's son

Botticelli himself, glancing towards the painting's viewer

The Church

By ABOUT 1500, there was growing unease about abuses within the Church. Many people believed that some Church leaders were more interested in making money than providing spiritual leadership. To raise the cash to support increasingly lavish lifestyles, some clergymen engaged in a number of corrupt practices, including the sale of "indulgences", papers that were believed to grant forgiveness of sins. This unease was to split the Christian world in an upheaval we call the Reformation, which led to the creation of the Protestant Church.

WEARING WEALTH
The ostentatious use of the Church's riches was not confined to popes and cardinals. This splendid necklace was probably worn by a Florentine priest. It is made of gilded bronze inset with precious and semi-precious stones with pictures of the Virgin Mary and baby Jesus in mother-of-pearl.

Sapphire

Dolphin emblem

HUGUENOT SLAUGHTER
By the 1550s, almost half of Europe had become Protestant. In response, the Catholic Church launched its own Counter-Reformation to restore Catholic influence. A century of religious wars followed. In France, fear of the growing Huguenot (French Protestant) community prompted a massacre on St Bartholomew's Day, 24 August, 1572, in which more than 3,000 Huguenots were slaughtered by mobs.

HAMMER OF FATE
In 1517, German monk Martin Luther (1483–1546) nailed a list of 95 criticisms of the Church to the door of Wittenberg Castle Church. His protests included the infamous sale of indulgences. The Church placed Luther under a ban, but his ideas spread quickly across Germany and throughout Europe, and the *Ninety-five Theses* became the spark that lit the Reformation fuse.

CARRY ON PATRON
Despite religious wars, the Church continued to commission works from great artists. One of the most stupendous was Michelangelo's enormous fresco on the ceiling of the Sistine Chapel in the Vatican, Rome. This detail shows a Sibyl (prophetess) from classical Greece.

Removable lid for inserting incense

CENSER STYLE
During Catholic mass, the air was rich with the smoke and sweet smell of incense. It was burned in censers, which altar boys carried to the priest. The practice was adopted from the religions of ancient Greece and Rome.

GLORY IN GLAZE

The patronage of the Church encouraged new artistic techniques. Among these was the use of glazed earthenware, pioneered by sculptor Luca della Robbia in about 1441. For nearly 75 years Luca's formula remained the secret of his family workshop. His great-nephew Giovanni used this technique to create this ornate Nativity altarpiece in 1521.

BATTLE OF PICTURES

This anti-Catholic medal depicts the pope as Satan. Following the Reformation, Catholics and Protestants waged a war of pamphlets and pictures, with each side portraying the other as evil or at least misled.

Intricate metalwork

ue was e colour of vinity and aven

herub with s hands asped in ayer

God the Father watches from heaven. The Protestants believed that depicting God in human form was blasphemous

Angels announce the birth of Christ in song

23

The new architecture

"WHOEVER WANTS TO BUILD in Italy today", said an Italian writer in the 1490s, "must turn to Florence for architects." At that time Florence boasted some of the most exciting and original buildings in Europe. Most adventurous of all was Brunelleschi's enormous dome for the city cathedral, which was completed in 1436. Spanning 39 m (130 ft), it was the largest domed structure built since the Pantheon was erected in Greece in C.E. 125.

Alberti's symbol of the blazing sun

MARVEL IN MARBLE
The church of Santa Maria Novella was built by Dominican monks in the late Middle Ages. In 1456, Leon Battista Alberti (1404–72) was commissioned to complete the stunning black-and-white marble facade. He added most of the upper section; harmonizing with the original design yet incorporating classical ideas of proportion and symmetry. Imaginary lines from the sun symbol to each corner of the base form an equal-sided triangle.

LIFTING TACKLE
In the building of the dome, heavy blocks of stone had to be lifted 40 m (131 ft) from the ground. Brunelleschi invented a mechanical hoist, which used ropes running through these pulleys.

A WHITEWASH
Not all Renaissance work represented an improvement. Originally, the interior walls of Santa Maria Novella were painted with frescoes. But in the 1560s, Giorgio Vasari (1511–74) was hired to modernize the church, and he covered the walls with whitewash. However, the interior's most notable feature can still be seen – the nave piers are spaced closer together at the east end, where the altar sits, to create an illusion of greater length.

The weight of the lantern helps to stabilize the structure of the entire dome

Globe weighs over 2 tonnes

INVENTIVE DESIGNER
Filippo Brunelleschi (1377–1446) was a goldsmith and sculptor before he turned to architecture.

PHILIPPI BRVNELLESCHI FLORENTINI ARCHITECTI CELEBERRIM EFFIGIES OB·AN·SAL·M·CCCCXLIII

ABOVE THEM ALL
Brunelleschi's dome was said to have inaugurated the Renaissance in Italy, and his fame and influence spread throughout the country.

Dome still towers over the city

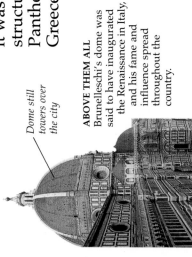

FINISHING TOUCH
The lantern that caps the dome is adorned with a copper globe. It was cast in Andrea del Verrocchio's workshop, where Leonardo was an apprentice, in 1471. The globe was raised up with a special machine that was probably built with Leonardo's help.

DECORATING THE INTERIOR
Brunelleschi planned to have the interior of the dome lined with gilt, while Lorenzo de' Medici wanted to have it covered with a vast mosaic.

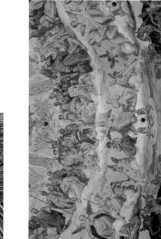

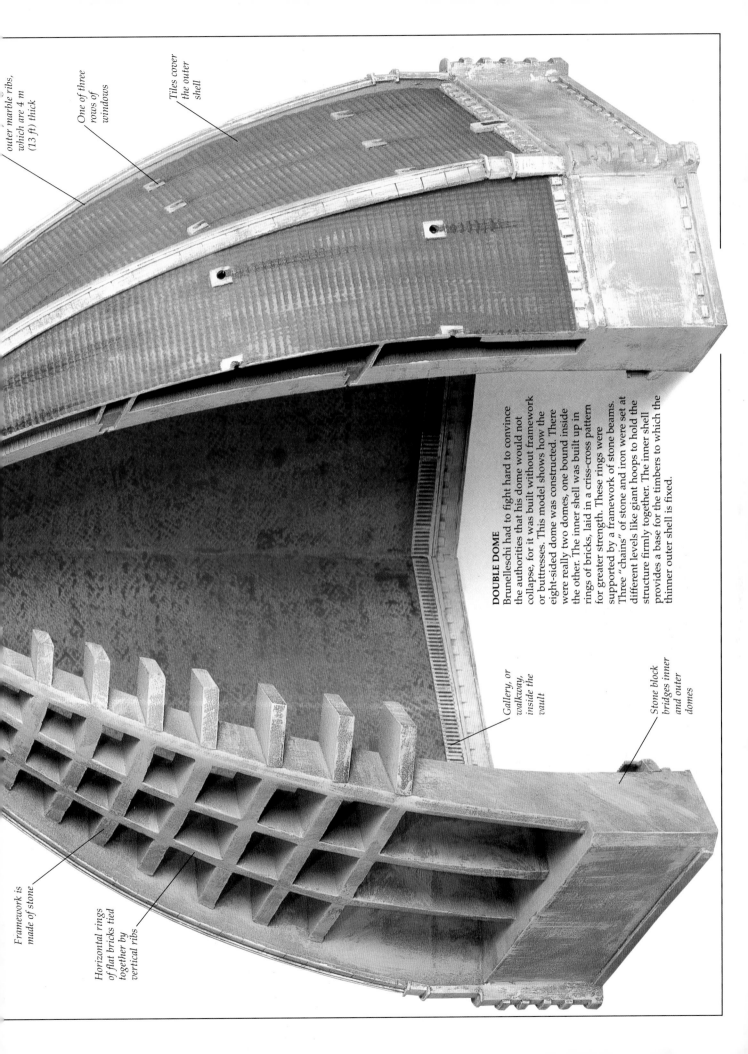

outer marble ribs, which are 4 m (13 ft) thick

One of three rows of windows

Tiles cover the outer shell

DOUBLE DOME
Brunelleschi had to fight hard to convince the authorities that his dome would not collapse, for it was built without framework or buttresses. This model shows how the eight-sided dome was constructed. There were really two domes, one bound inside the other. The inner shell was built up in rings of bricks, laid in a criss-cross pattern for greater strength. These rings were supported by a framework of stone beams. Three "chains" of stone and iron were set at different levels like giant hoops to hold the structure firmly together. The inner shell provides a base for the timbers to which the thinner outer shell is fixed.

Gallery, or walkway, inside the vault

Stone block bridges inner and outer domes

Framework is made of stone

Horizontal rings of flat bricks tied together by vertical ribs

The workshop

EARLY RENAISSANCE ARTISTS were regarded as craftsmen, and their methods of work were strictly controlled by their guilds or trade associations. They learned their trade in busy workshops, which were run by master craftsmen who obtained commissions for them to work on. For the first year, an apprentice practised drawing, then spent several years learning essential tasks such as making brushes, grinding pigments, preparing wood panels, and handling gold leaf.

Quill

Sab brus

Squirrel-fur brushes

MAKING BRUSHES
To make soft-hair brushes, the apprentice tied together bunches of hairs from the tail tips of an ermine, or stoat. This animal i related to the Russian sable, whose fur is used for high-quality brushes nowadays. The apprentice fitted each bunch to a short piece of quill, and inserted a wooden handle. The harder bristle brushes were made of white pig's bristles, which were softened by whitewashing walls with them before painting.

Pestle and mortar would have been made of hard wood, such as this one, or stone

Pestle and mortar

Hog's-hair brushes

DAILY GRIND
Apprentices had to keep up a steady supply of stock paints. Paints were made by crushing pigments in a pestle and mortar. The resulting powder was then mixed with a binding medium, such as egg yolk for tempera painting, or a slow-drying oil, such as walnut or linseed oil, for oil painting.

Gesso

Bitumen

LADY WITH ERMINE
This portrait by Leonardo shows Cecilia Gallerani (mistress of Lodovico Sforza, Duke of Milan) holding a pet ermine with a white winter coat (as used in brush-making). An ermine was one of Lodovico's emblems, and the animal is also probably intended as a visual pun on Cecilia Gallerani's name – *gale* is the Greek name for an ermine. Leonardo has enlarged the ermine and the woman's hand very slightly to give balance to the overall composition.

GESSO LAYERING
Panels and canvases were covered with layers of gesso, made of a soft mineral called gypsum, before painting or gilding.

UNDERPAINTING
Bitumen brown was used by artists such as Leonardo for underpainting; it helped define light and shade.

The texture of the ermine's fur is rendered in oil paint, using the finest brushwork

PREPARING A PANEL

One of the apprentice's jobs was to prepare wood panels for painting. Poplar, oak (as shown here), or silver fir were considered the most suitable woods. First, the apprentice boiled the bare wood in water to prevent it from splitting. Next, the panel was coated with size, a clear glue made from boiled animal skins. Then it was coated with gesso to give it an even surface for painting.

Yellow lake

Verdaccio

Cinabrese

Sinoper

Buckthorn berries

THE FINISHED PANEL
This original panel is the reverse of Leonardo's famous portrait of Florentine lady Ginevra de' Benci. Leonardo has decorated the back of the panel with a Latin motto meaning "beauty adorns virtue", a compliment to Ginevra.

PAINTS FOR FLESH
For painting flesh in egg tempera, layering of colour was required. An underpaint of verdaccio was worked over with sinoper and cinabrese.

BERRIES AND BEETLES
Some coloured glazes were made from organic materials mixed with powdered chalk and a binding agent. Buckthorn berries produced a delicate colour called yellow lake. Cochineal insects produced carmine, which was made into a vivid crimson glaze for oil painting.

Carmine

Cochineal beetles

ART TO ORDER
Here, a young apprentice crushes minerals for pigments. Only when he had mastered such tasks would the apprentice be allowed to work on a painting. However, by the end of his training, he was expected to be skilled in a wide variety of techniques. A workshop commonly produced a range of items, from portraits and statues to painted furniture and ceremonial armour.

Azurite

Ultramarine

Lapis lazuli

PRICEY PIGMENT
Rich ultramarine blue was widely used in Renaissance painting. To make this pigment, the apprentice ground lapis lazuli, a semi-precious stone, to a powder. Ultramarine means "from across the seas", as the pigment had to be shipped from Afghanistan. A cheaper blue pigment could be extracted from azurite.

Making a panel for an altarpiece

CHURCHES OF THE 15TH CENTURY HAD MANY ALTARS, each of which was usually adorned with an altarpiece. The largest and most important altar was the high altar at the end of the nave. This was the focal point of the church. Painted altarpieces might consist of a single large panel or several smaller panels illustrating sacred themes, and set in elaborate frames. Some altarpieces were huge, fixed structures that might also incorporate sculptures. Tiny, transportable altarpieces were sometimes owned by wealthy individuals.

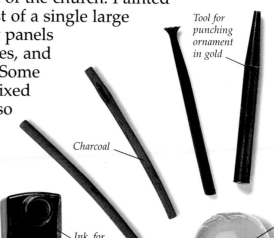

Tool for punching ornament in gold

Charcoal

Ink, for fixing outlines

Egg yolk, for tempera painting

Unprepared bole

Array of materials used in panel decoration

GLOWING GOLD
The gold leaf of the altarpiece shone out gloriously from the general gloom of the church. An altarpiece was designed to make worshippers gasp in awe at its spiritual splendour; it was also a dramatic way of displaying the wealth and piety of whoever had paid for it – the community, a local patron, or a trade guild.

PREPARING THE PANEL
The technique of decorating a panel for an altarpiece is described in detail by Cennino Cennini, a 14th-century Tuscan painter. First, the artist prepared the wooden panel by brushing on a ground made up of layers of white gesso. This was then scraped and polished until it was completely smooth, "like ivory". On this, he drew the design with charcoal. When he was happy with his sketch, he fixed the outlines with a soft brush dipped in diluted black ink.

PREPARING FOR GILDING
Using a stylus, or sharp tool, the artist lightly scored divisions between areas of the work to be gilded and those to be painted. Next, he prepared a special cushioned surface on which to lay the gold leaf. This was made of bole, a kind of soft clay, which was ground, mixed with whisked egg white (called glair), and then brushed on. Layers of the bole mixture were applied to the surface and carefully smoothed with a brush to stop them from cracking.

Boled area is an earthy red and gives the gold a rich, warm colour

GILDING THE PANEL

Gold leaf is so thin that it is difficult to control and can easily blow away in a draught. In Cennini's day, it was handled with a piece of card. Nowadays, a special brush called a gilder's tip is used. To make sure there were no tiny gaps, each piece of gold leaf slightly overlapped the previous one. Only when the gold leaf had been burnished and decorated could the artist begin painting.

Parchment, to stop the gold leaf from blowing away

Diluted bole with brush

Burnisher with agate tip

Gesso ground

Bole

Burnished gold leaf

Unburnished gold leaf

NOT FADE AWAY

Gold leaf was made by beating gold into progressively thinner sheets. It was perfect material for decoration, because it does not rust or tarnish.

PAINTING THE PANEL

This illustration from a French manuscript of 1403 shows a woman painting a panel. Her assistant is grinding up pigments ready to be bound with egg. Until the mid-15th century, artists usually painted panels with egg tempera (powdered pigment mixed with egg yolk), using fine ermine and squirrel hair brushes.

¹URNISHING AND DECORATING

'hen gold leaf was first applied, it ¹peared crumpled and matt. To make ³hine, it had to be burnished. For ¹s, the artist used a perfectly ¹ooth piece of stone mounted on a ¹ck. The stone might be semi- ¹ecious, such as agate, or precious, ¹ch as sapphire or emerald. The artist ¹rted by gently rubbing the burnisher ¹r the gold, gradually pressing ¹rder until it was burnished to a ¹h, reflective gleam. The circles of ¹ haloes, as in the picture above, ¹re inscribed with dividers or ¹ompass. Further designs ¹ght be inscribed with punching tools.

Agate

Sapphire

Dividers

Emerald

Taming the wilderness

DURING THE 15TH CENTURY, the wealthy families of Italy began spending their summers in the countryside. To escape the noise, overcrowding, and threat of plague in the cities, they built elegant villas in the landscape near Florence, Rome, and Venice. By the mid-16th century large areas of bare hillside were being transformed into stunning formal gardens, planted with exotic trees and thousands of flowers. At the same time, landscapes and scenes of country life started to become fashionable subjects for paintings. The idea of the country as a retreat from the strain of city life was the beginning of an attitude that is still common among city-dwellers today.

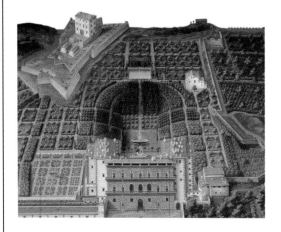

GRAND GARDENS
The huge Boboli Gardens in Florence were laid out by the Medici in 1550. The ground was flattened, then planted with firs, cypresses, and laurels in complex geometric patterns. The dip behind the palace was an amphitheatre, based on an ancient Roman circus.

IMPROVING ON NATURE
Leonardo was fascinated by the flow of water, and he drew up several projects for altering the course of the River Arno, which flows through Florence. One, shown here, proposed digging three new channels to cut off a bend in the river and improve its flow. In 1503, work was begun to divert the Arno, based on Leonardo's proposals. Although the scheme eventually failed, a modern anti-flooding project resembles his original plans.

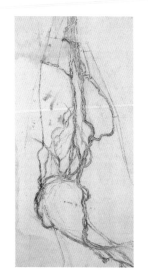

Boats on the river, shown as single lines

THE FIRST LANDSCAPE
The Tuscan countryside of Leonardo's childhood was the subject of his earliest known drawing, dated 1473. The countryside was not yet considered a suitable subject for art, and this has been called "the first landscape drawing in Western art". Every feature of the scene, including trees bending in the wind, is faithfully reproduced.

PALLADIAN VILLA
Architect Andrea Palladio (1508–80) designed the Villa Barbarosa, below, for a rich Venetian family. He based his buildings (most of which are in or around his native city of Vicenza) on classical Greek and Roman models, making use of temple columns and pediments, and emphasizing symmetry and proportion.

Matching wings each contain three groups of three rooms

Classical statues adorn the courtyard

LOVE OF NATURE
Leonardo's notebooks are crammed with studies of animals and plants, such as this red chalk drawing of an oak branch with acorns. He was fascinated by the natural world, and felt so tenderly about animals that he would buy caged birds in order to set them free.

Acorn sprig

QUEST FOR KNOWLEDGE
Unlike medieval artists, Leonardo drew his plants directly from nature. This sketch of a star-of-Bethlehem flower was a study for a larger work. His interest was partly scientific, for he was eager to examine the structures and life systems of plants, and he made detailed notes about what he drew.

Star-of-Bethlehem

USTIC REALITIES
his 1530 fresco, from an Italian castle, shows grapes eing harvested and crushed to make wine. There is o indication of hardship here, although in reality ost European peasants lived in extreme poverty. heir harsh lives were often idealized in paintings at decorated the country villas of the rich.

Portico, with pillars and pediment like a Greek temple

Regularly arcaded front walls

Proportion and perspective

THE ARTISTS OF THE RENAISSANCE learned from the ancient Greeks that ideals of beauty and harmony were governed by mathematical principles. For painters, the challenge was perspective; how to represent a three-dimensional image on a flat surface. Brunelleschi showed that if lines are drawn on a two-dimensional surface and made to converge at a "vanishing point", they give the illusion of space and distance. Alberti, Leonardo, and others used his theories to explore further the role of geometry and mathematics in art. Sculptors strove to create beautiful and harmonious figures by studying the ideal proportions of the human body. Architects experimented with the principles of symmetry, geometry, and proportion – often with surprising results.

MAN OF PARTS
Leon Battista Alberti – architect, mathematician, playwright, and musician – set out the rules of perspective in his treatise *On Painting*.

Giambologna's *Mercury* viewed from four angl

AMUSEMENT ARCADE
The principles of perspective can be used to create practical jokes. In 1652, Francesco Borromini designed this "perspective arcade" for a courtyard in Rome. The arcade is real enough, but much shallower than it looks – it is only 8.5 m (28 ft) in length. The illusion of depth is achieved by making columns and ceiling panels smaller as they recede. The floor slopes upwards and its apparently square patterns are in fact trapezoid.

Net is placed close to model for a foreshortened pose

DRAWING THE NET
To help him create perspective in his drawings, Alberti devised a "net". The idea was developed by the German artist Albrecht Dürer in 1525. The net was a square network of black threads stretched on a wooden frame. The artist placed an eyepiece at a fixed distance from the object he was drawing. He then looked over the eyepiece and through the net, and reproduced the outlines of the model onto a sheet of paper with squares corresponding to the network on the frame.

Stretched silk threads

Pointing finger stresses upward motion

Winged helmet

Staff with two entwined snakes

Elongated, elegant body

Swivelled hips emphasize movement

IN THE ROUND
This bronze statue by Giambologna (1529–1608), court sculptor to the Medici, is of the classical Roman messenger god, Mercury. The statue is based on the geometric form of the coil, spiralling upwards. This accounts for the perfect proportions of the figure, viewed from any angle. Giambologna was influenced by the work of his near contemporary Michelangelo, as well as by classical ideas of proportion and symmetry. He imbued his *Mercury* with a new sense of vibrant movement and inner tension.

Winged heel

Entire statue poised on the point of one foot

Mercury balances on a column of air coming from the mouth of a wind god

LEONARDO'S *LAST SUPPER*
In about 1495, Leonardo began work on a vast wall mural, *The Last Supper*, for a monastery in Milan, which he had to paint from scaffolding. An eyewitness described how, in spite of this inconvenience, Leonardo would work from dawn to dusk, "never laying down the brush, but continuing to paint without remembering to eat or drink". Unfortunately, the painting started to deteriorate even in Leonardo's lifetime and has since become seriously damaged.

The vanishing point, where the lines converge

POINT OF VIEW
The Last Supper was placed high above eye level. Leonardo made clever use of linear perspective to lift the viewer up to the correct viewpoint. He achieved this by perspective pull – which draws the spectator's eye towards Christ's head.

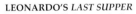
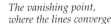

THE POWER OF PERSPECTIVE
Leonardo's painting is high on the wall of the monk's dining room. Leonardo has painted Christ in slightly larger scale than the disciples, and his head is framed by light from a window behind him. These techniques had the effect of making the monks aware of Christ's presence as they ate at their own table below.

Renaissance rivals

IN APRIL 1500, LEONARDO returned to Florence after long years of service in Milan. He was already a celebrated genius, not only in painting but also in engineering. However, he left several embarrassing failures behind him, including an over-ambitious design for an equestrian statue in bronze. Back in Florence, Leonardo encountered another great genius, Michelangelo, who mocked him about the unfinished statue. Leonardo was deeply hurt, and the incident caused a rift between the two. Their rivalry was put the test in 1504, when both artists were commissioned to produce major murals for the great council hall in the refurbished Palazzo Vecchio. The careers of other great figures of the Renaissance were also marked by rivalry and competition.

BATTLE CRY
Leonardo and Michelangelo were asked to commemorate two recent Florentine military victories – at Anghiari and at Cascina. In 1364 the Pisan army had been defeated by the Florentines at Cascina, and in 1440 the Florentine army had crushed Milanese mercenary troops at Anghiari. For the Anghiari painting, Leonardo studied old records of battles and made preliminary sketches for the characters involved, such as this shouting soldier.

FIGHT FOR THE FLAG
Leonardo's rough sketch for the middle section of the *Battle of Anghiari* shows soldiers fighting to seize the enemy's standard (flag). Here, he is experimenting with the shapes of men and horses under the extreme conditions of battle.

RUBENS' RECORD
Alas, neither Leonardo nor Michelangelo finished their commissions. After careful planning, Leonardo started on the central panel of the *Battle of Anghiari*. But he could not resist experimenting. To heighten the brilliance of his colours, he painted onto a surface of plaster coated with a resinous substance called pitch (a recipe copied from the classical writer Pliny). Disastrously, the paint would not dry. Leonardo had a fire lit at the base of the wall, but the colours on the upper part ran, leaving a hopeless mess. Today, there is no trace of the work. The only record is this copy made in 1603 by the Flemish painter Peter Paul Rubens (1577–1640) from a Leonardo engraving.

THE CONTRACT
Artists were given contracts by their employers for major commissions. Like this one, the documents usually gave strict instructions about materials and subject matter. There might also be penalty clauses in case the work was late or left incomplete.

UNFINISHED MASTERPIECE
Michelangelo started on the cartoon (preparatory drawing for a fresco) for the *Battle of Cascina* late in 1504, while Leonardo was working on his drawing. For once, both great artists were in harmony. In March 1505, the two cartoons were put on display. Then Michelangelo was summoned to Rome by the pope, and he never completed his mural. The cartoon was eventually lost. Luckily, Michelangelo's friend Aristotile da Sangallo made this copy in about 1542.

Aristotile's copy of Michelangelo's figure

Figure is poised to flee

FROZEN MOVEMENT
A few of Michelangelo's drawings for the *Battle of Cascina* survive. Like this sketch, they show naked soldiers struggling to respond to the threat of danger. The figures twist and turn, their muscles tense. The Aristotile picture (left) shows how the artist used this particular figure in the cartoon.

Panel shows the sacrifice of Isaac

Frenzied horse tramples soldier

Ghiberti's winning door panel

Brunelleschi's door panel

Replica doors at the Florence Baptistery are shown below – the originals are kept in a museum

Ghiberti's self-portrait in the doorframe

COMPETITION PANELS
In 1401, a competition was held in Florence among seven leading artists to decide who should design new doors for the baptistery. The prize was awarded to Lorenzo Ghiberti (1378–1455). Brunelleschi was asked to collaborate with Ghiberti, but he refused, declaring that he would become an architect instead.

THE GATES OF PARADISE
Ghiberti was to spend much of the rest of his career making two pairs of bronze doors for the Florence Baptistery. The East doors (which took 27 years to complete) contain ten panels, each showing Old Testament scenes in relief. Michelangelo called them "the gates of paradise".

Fashion and finery

DURING THE RENAISSANCE, clothes became even more significant as a sign of wealth and status than they had been in the Middle Ages. Luxury fabrics, such as silks and furs, were widely available. And more importance was attached to dress in Italy than elsewhere in Europe. The wealthy couldn't resist showing off the fine fabrics that their craftsmen produced, as well as extravagant imported materials. Rich families dressed their servants in lavish clothes too, so that the whole household would give an impression of wealth. Both Venice and Florence passed sumptuary laws, which restricted the wearing of luxurious clothing to specific classes of society. These laws were unpopular and hard to enforce. But in cities without sumptuary laws, it was noted that "no difference can be observed between noble and burgher".

HAIR TODAY, GONE TOMORROW
Men's hair fashions changed bewilderingly during the Renaissance. When this picture of an armed warrior was painted, in about 1500, men favoured long hair and a clean-shaven chin. By the 1520s, the fashion had switched to short hair plus beards and moustaches. By 1600, hair was long again, but long beards were laughed at.

16th-century ivory comb

COMBS AND CURL
A Renaissance beaut would take great troub each day to arrange he hair. A wealthy woma would have had an ivo comb, such as the on above, and a special hai parting instrument. Gu arabic, used as a glue the 20th century, was use to make curls stick to t forehead! Thick strands hair were stiffened wi gold lacquer and calle "Venus's hai

Raw gum arabic

Plaits, or braids, twisted to form a figure-of-eight

A modern bottle of liquid gum arabic

Ivory hair-parting instruments

GIRL WITH DRESSED HAIR
"Among the simple minded, one single hair out of place means high disgrace," wrote Leonardo. This drawing by his teacher, Andrea del Verrocchio, shows every detail of the model's carefully arranged hair. The most fashionable colour for hair was blond, and many women tried to bleach their hair by spending whole days in the sun. False hair, made of white or yellow silk, was also popular, even though it was forbidden by law.

SIMPLE BEAUTY
With her well-balanced features, slightly pointed chin, and heavy eyelids, the face of the *Mona Lisa* represents Leonardo's vision of ideal beauty. Unlike the richly ornamented women painted by his contemporaries, she displays no jewellery and wears a simple dress and fine black veil. The *Mona Lisa*'s true identity has never been verified, and the meaning of her enigmatic smile continues to be debated.

PEARL BAN
This pendant is decorated with pearl drops. A Sienese sumptuary law forbade women to wear pearls – until the women's protests forced a reversal of the ban.

Cameo depicts the Adoration

LADY OF FASHION
Lavish wealth is displayed in almost every aspect of this portrait of Dona Margarita de Cardona by a follower of the Venetian painter Titian. Her collar is made of fur, and her headdress and necklaces are jewelled with pearls, sapphires, and rubies. Her sleeves are decorated with gold and silver embroidery.

Gilt belt, possibly a betrothal gift

ad
cklace
tches
acelets

IDEAL COUPLE
This silver gilt belt buckle was a betrothal gift. While many such gifts are decorated with portraits of the betrothed couple, this one shows an imaginary "ideal" couple.

LITTLE ADULT
This portrait is by Sofonisba Anguissola (c. 1527–1625), one of the first female artists to become famous. It shows a child looking rather uncomfortable in a bulky, embroidered tunic and lace ruff. Childhood was not regarded as a separate state from adulthood in Renaissance times, as it is today. Children were thought of as miniature adults, and were dressed in tiny versions of adults' clothes.

In the home

THE FAMILY HOME was the centre of life in Renaissance Europe. This was partly because the home often doubled up as a workplace. In the towns, craftsmen and shopkeepers worked in their own houses; in the country, peasants shared their homes with their animals during the winters. Servants and apprentices lived with their employers as family members. Many women, such as Leonardo's second step-mother, died in childbirth. When this happened, widowers often re-married, and more family members joined the home. The husband was expected to rule the household, and his wife to attend to the day-to-day running of the home.

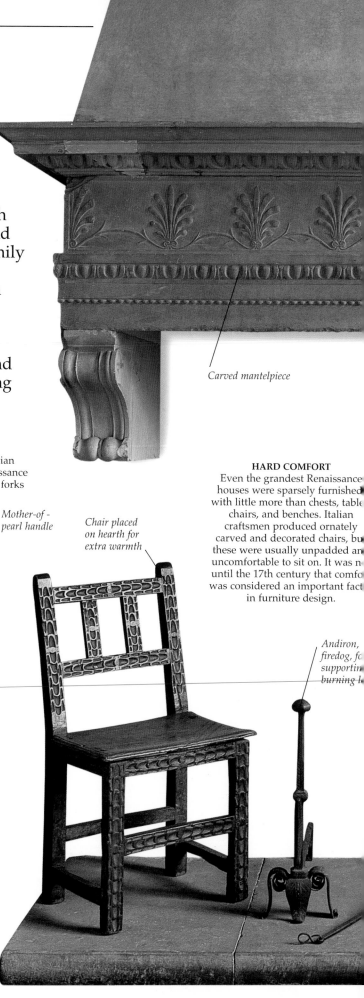

Carved mantelpiece

Two-pronged fork for skewering meat

Italian Renaissance table forks

Plain, four-pronged fork

Mother-of-pearl handle

Chair placed on hearth for extra warmth

FORK LIFT
Table forks were rare in medieval times, when people used knives and fingers to eat. By the early 15th century, forks had been introduced to Italy from Byzantium and the East. Soon, elaborately decorated forks were being used in wealthier homes. However, forks did not catch on in northern Europe until more than a century later.

HARD COMFORT
Even the grandest Renaissance houses were sparsely furnished with little more than chests, tables, chairs, and benches. Italian craftsmen produced ornately carved and decorated chairs, but these were usually unpadded and uncomfortable to sit on. It was not until the 17th century that comfort was considered an important factor in furniture design.

Andiron, firedog, for supporting burning l...

FAMILY LIFE
Leonardo's earliest home was this simple house at Anchiano, near Vinci. He was the illegitimate son of a peasant girl and a local notary (official). He was brought up in his father's home in a typical extended family, which included a succession of stepmothers and sixteen half-brothers and sisters.

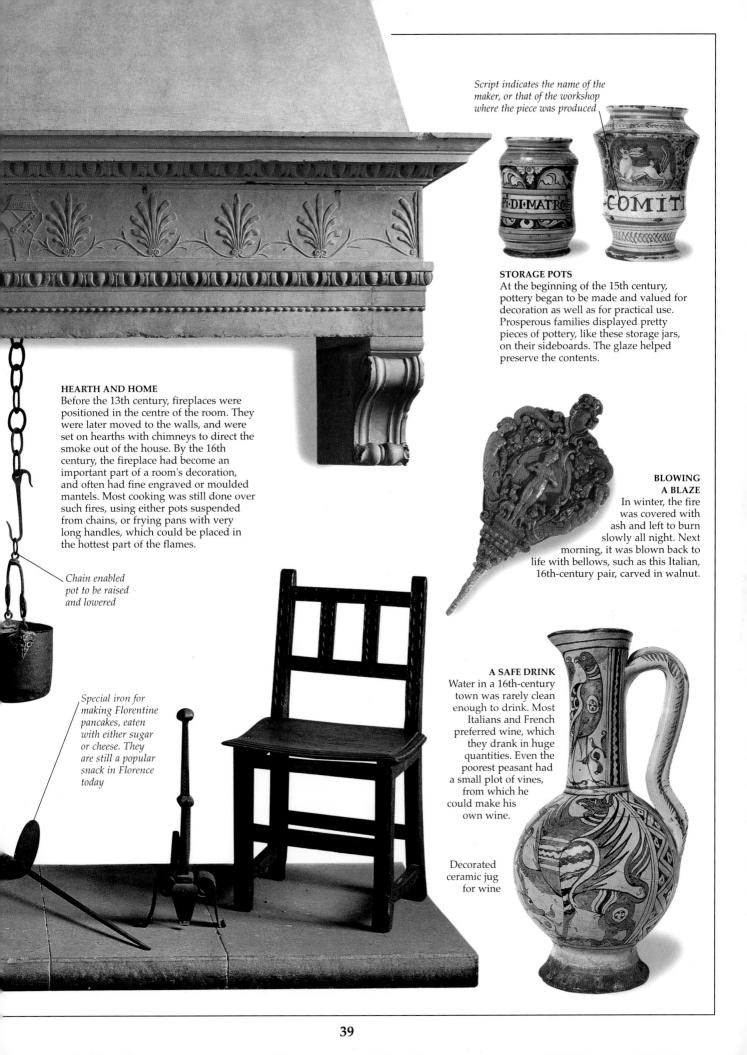

Script indicates the name of the maker, or that of the workshop where the piece was produced

PI·DI·MATRO

COMITI

STORAGE POTS
At the beginning of the 15th century, pottery began to be made and valued for decoration as well as for practical use. Prosperous families displayed pretty pieces of pottery, like these storage jars, on their sideboards. The glaze helped preserve the contents.

HEARTH AND HOME
Before the 13th century, fireplaces were positioned in the centre of the room. They were later moved to the walls, and were set on hearths with chimneys to direct the smoke out of the house. By the 16th century, the fireplace had become an important part of a room's decoration, and often had fine engraved or moulded mantels. Most cooking was still done over such fires, using either pots suspended from chains, or frying pans with very long handles, which could be placed in the hottest part of the flames.

Chain enabled pot to be raised and lowered

BLOWING A BLAZE
In winter, the fire was covered with ash and left to burn slowly all night. Next morning, it was blown back to life with bellows, such as this Italian, 16th-century pair, carved in walnut.

Special iron for making Florentine pancakes, eaten with either sugar or cheese. They are still a popular snack in Florence today

A SAFE DRINK
Water in a 16th-century town was rarely clean enough to drink. Most Italians and French preferred wine, which they drank in huge quantities. Even the poorest peasant had a small plot of vines, from which he could make his own wine.

Decorated ceramic jug for wine

Design for living

Renaissance homes were more comfortable than draughty medieval halls, but they were relatively sparse by modern standards. Practical, domestic items were frequently inefficient or awkward to use. However, the increase of private patronage encouraged a new awareness of design, and there were improvements – especially for the well-off. Battista Alberti noted that the accumulation of beautiful possessions was a principal preoccupation of family life. Better, and more elaborate, lamps and candle holders gave out more light. Silvered mirrors on the walls reflected the light, as well as the images of those who looked into them. Carved wooden furniture became more elegant, and the development of the mechanical clock meant that the 24 hours of the day could now be measured accurately.

PINCH OF SNUFFER
There were only two ways of lighting a room – with oil lamps and candles. Vegetable or mineral oil was burned in small vessels using a fibre wick. Candles were made of tallow (animal fat) or beeswax, which was much more expensive. The candles were extinguished with metal snuffers, such as this elegant pair.

Open fretwork to let out smoke from candle

NIGHTLIGHT
In the Middle Ages, most lamps and candle holders were simple in design. From the late 15th century, more decorative lighting systems came into use. In 1490, Leonardo designed an oil lamp with a glass chimney. This gilded bronze and enamel candle container was made in Venice in the 16th century. Its elaborate decoration is typical of later Renaissance design.

Intricately carved ivory surround – the mirror is highly ornamental as well as practical

NEW REFLECTIONS
Glass was coarse and discoloured until the craftsmen of Venice discovered how to make a clear product, called *cristallo*, in the 1400s. This important advance led to the manufacture of silvered mirrors. For the first time in history, people could see true reflections of themselves. They became more aware of their appearance, and of new fashions in cosmetics, clothes, and hairstyles. Artists also used mirrors to paint self-portraits.

Mirrors of this period had convex glass, which is distorting

LETTING IN LIGHT

Until the late 17th century, glass makers could produce only small panes of flat glass. In a window such as this one, from a 15th-century Florentine palace, the panes were held together with lead. Heavy wooden shutters were used in place of curtains – they kept rooms warm in winter and cool in summer. Such shutters are still used instead of curtains in Italy, and in other Mediterranean countries. Glass windows and wooden shutters were very expensive, however, and poor people had to make do with draughty oiled paper, parchment, or canvas.

Naturally impure glass is slightly coloured

SAVONAROLA CHAIR

In the cramped space of a study or monk's cell, furniture had to be easily stored. This 16th-century chair could be folded and leant against the wall. It was called a Savonarola chair, after the Florentine monk who used one. The chair was both practical and elegant, with a semi-circular design that actually originated in ancient Roman times.

Curved legs fit inside one another when folded

A SNIP

Large bronze or iron shears were invented in pre-classical times. But it was not until the 16th century that small scissors appeared, making tasks such as cutting hair and sewing much easier.

Gilded fretwork lid

POCKET WATCH

Early clocks, driven by a falling weight, kept poor time. In the 16th century, the invention of the coiled spring made it possible to produce much more accurate clocks, as well as portable watches, like this brass one. Such watches were worn on a chain around the neck, as much for decoration as for timekeeping.

DEADLY LOCKETS

These pretty pendants may have contained either a lock of a loved one's hair – or a dose of poison, intended for any potential enemies.

PLATFORMS

The first platform shoes, called *zoccoli*, were made in 16th-century Venice. These wooden shoes initially had a practical purpose – to keep feet dry in the flooded Venetian streets, but they soon became fashion items. Women were supported by servants as they tottered about on the elevated shoes, which rose as high as 76 cm (30 in). In spite of their impracticality, platform shoes became fashionable again in Europe during the 20th century.

The human body

FOR 1,000 YEARS, the science of the body – anatomy – had remained virtually unchanged. Medieval doctors relied on textbooks and tradition. In the 16th century, a revolution in anatomy took place, led by artists (most notably Leonardo and Michelangelo) as well as doctors. This revolution, inspired by the rediscovery of the writings of the great classical physicians, and encouraged by a new spirit of enquiry and observation, changed everything. Both doctors and artists began to dissect bodies and to describe the results with unheard-of accuracy. Consequently, the work of artists and anatomists during the Renaissance is sometimes remarkably similar.

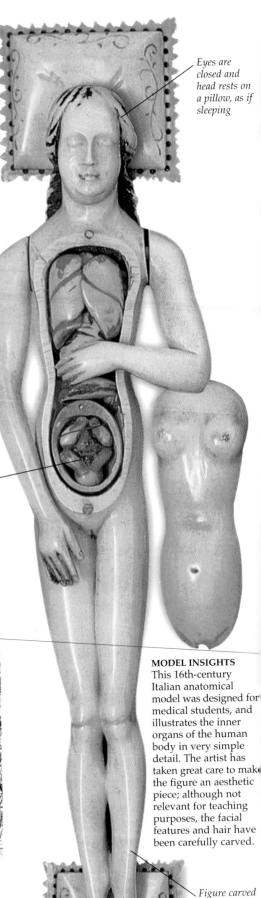

Eyes are closed and head rests on a pillow, as if sleeping

Digestive system

MODEL INSIGHTS
This 16th-century Italian anatomical model was designed for medical students, and illustrates the inner organs of the human body in very simple detail. The artist has taken great care to make the figure an aesthetic piece; although not relevant for teaching purposes, the facial features and hair have been carefully carved.

Figure carved from ivory

THE PERFECT BODY
Renaissance artists, particularly in Florence, followed the classical example by basing their work on the nude figure. Michelangelo's massive statue *David* uses an intimate knowledge of bone structure, muscles, sinews, and veins to express the body's grace and nobility.

Title page showing a public dissection

TEACHING REVOLUTION
De Humani Corporis Fabrica (Fabric of the Human Body) by the Flemish physician Andreas Vesalius (1514–64) had a profound influence on medicine. Before its publication in 1543, medical students were taught from textbooks written over a millennium earlier, which were based on out-dated theories rather than the practice of human dissection.

BATH-HOUSE BODIES
Early Renaissance sculptors and painters had limited opportunity for observing the naked human body. The medieval Church discouraged the depiction of nude figures, and most rediscovered classical nudes were in Rome. Not surprisingly, some artists made discreet use of public bath-houses, such as this establishment, which were shared between the sexes.

CUT TO THE HEART

John Banister, a pioneering British anatomist, is shown here lecturing in London, England in 1581. Human dissection had been restricted because the Church believed the practice was disrespectful to God. However, restrictions were finally lifted by the 16th century, and anatomy became an essential part of a doctor's training.

Internal organs are displayed

Saw, used for amputations

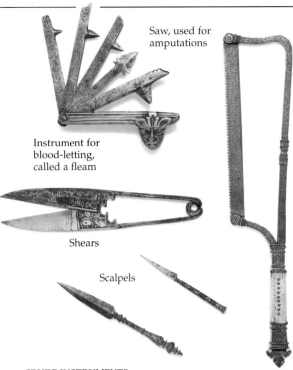

Instrument for blood-letting, called a fleam

Shears

Scalpels

BLOOD AND BONES

Skull made to pivot

This strange, robot-like model was used to teach bone-setting. It was probably designed by Italian anatomist Hieronymous Fabricius (1537–1619). He also devised operations for correcting spinal deformities, and made important discoveries about blood vessels. Fabricius taught with Vesalius at the anatomical school at Padua, Italy's centre for the new anatomical science.

CRUDE INSTRUMENTS

Before the 16th century, surgeons were considered little more than mechanics. They had scant training, and often doubled as travelling barbers. Their array of instruments was often unsterilized and crude, as above. But the French surgeon Ambroise Paré (1510–90), known as "the father of modern surgery", helped to improve standards. Paré closed wounds by stitching, rather than cauterizing, them.

MORGUE NIGHTS

Leonardo was determined to form a complete picture of how the systems of the human body fit together. To achieve this, he dissected 30 bodies of men and women in the local morgue. The experience of "living through the night hours in the company of these corpses, quartered and flayed and horrible to behold," as he described it, made studies such as this one possible.

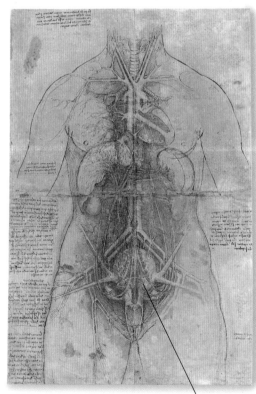

Metal knee joints

Ankle joints

The artist's detailed notes on his observations

Uterus (womb)

TURNING THE ARM

"Human movement may be understood through knowledge of the parts of the body," wrote Leonardo. This study shows the action of the muscles in a man's arm and shoulder. The sequence shows the arms from several slightly different viewpoints.

Dreams of flying

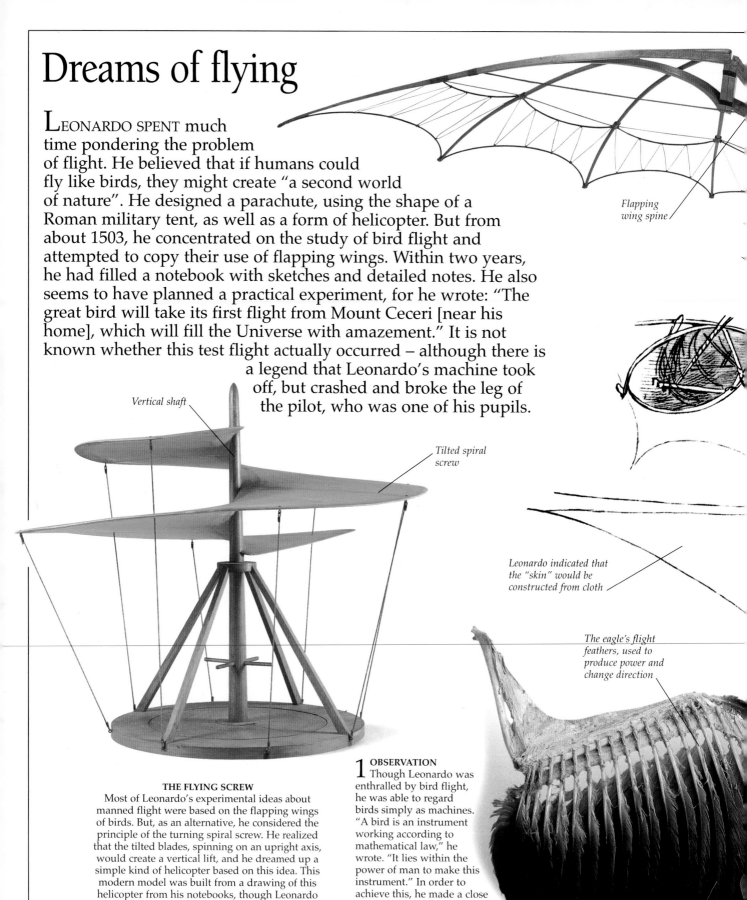

LEONARDO SPENT much time pondering the problem of flight. He believed that if humans could fly like birds, they might create "a second world of nature". He designed a parachute, using the shape of a Roman military tent, as well as a form of helicopter. But from about 1503, he concentrated on the study of bird flight and attempted to copy their use of flapping wings. Within two years, he had filled a notebook with sketches and detailed notes. He also seems to have planned a practical experiment, for he wrote: "The great bird will take its first flight from Mount Ceceri [near his home], which will fill the Universe with amazement." It is not known whether this test flight actually occurred – although there is a legend that Leonardo's machine took off, but crashed and broke the leg of the pilot, who was one of his pupils.

Flapping wing spine

Vertical shaft

Tilted spiral screw

Leonardo indicated that the "skin" would be constructed from cloth

The eagle's flight feathers, used to produce power and change direction

THE FLYING SCREW

Most of Leonardo's experimental ideas about manned flight were based on the flapping wings of birds. But, as an alternative, he considered the principle of the turning spiral screw. He realized that the tilted blades, spinning on an upright axis, would create a vertical lift, and he dreamed up a simple kind of helicopter based on this idea. This modern model was built from a drawing of this helicopter from his notebooks, though Leonardo gave no clue as to how the machine would be powered. However, his idea anticipated the use of the spinning propeller, which would eventually drive the first successful aircraft.

1 OBSERVATION
Though Leonardo was enthralled by bird flight, he was able to regard birds simply as machines. "A bird is an instrument working according to mathematical law," he wrote. "It lies within the power of man to make this instrument." In order to achieve this, he made a close examination of the structure of birds' wings. He noted that the eagle is a heavy creature, but its huge wingspan (about 2.5 m, or 8 ft) makes it supportable. Leonardo noted the strength and flexibility of the eagle's wings, and the way they curve slightly from front to back.

Secondary feathers form curve that provides lift

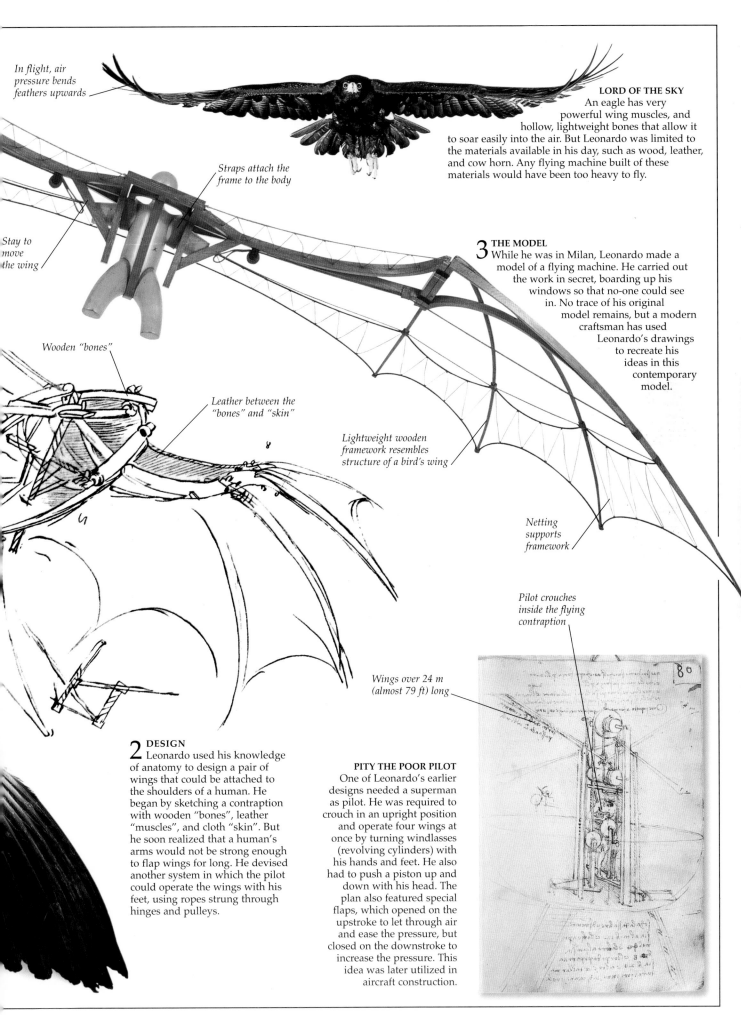

*In flight, air
pressure bends
feathers upwards*

LORD OF THE SKY
An eagle has very
powerful wing muscles, and
hollow, lightweight bones that allow it
to soar easily into the air. But Leonardo was limited to
the materials available in his day, such as wood, leather,
and cow horn. Any flying machine built of these
materials would have been too heavy to fly.

*Straps attach the
frame to the body*

*Stay to
move
the wing*

3 THE MODEL
While he was in Milan, Leonardo made a
model of a flying machine. He carried out
the work in secret, boarding up his
windows so that no-one could see
in. No trace of his original
model remains, but a modern
craftsman has used
Leonardo's drawings
to recreate his
ideas in this
contemporary
model.

Wooden "bones"

*Leather between the
"bones" and "skin"*

*Lightweight wooden
framework resembles
structure of a bird's wing*

*Netting
supports
framework*

*Pilot crouches
inside the flying
contraption*

*Wings over 24 m
(almost 79 ft) long*

2 DESIGN
Leonardo used his knowledge
of anatomy to design a pair of
wings that could be attached to
the shoulders of a human. He
began by sketching a contraption
with wooden "bones", leather
"muscles", and cloth "skin". But
he soon realized that a human's
arms would not be strong enough
to flap wings for long. He devised
another system in which the pilot
could operate the wings with his
feet, using ropes strung through
hinges and pulleys.

PITY THE POOR PILOT
One of Leonardo's earlier
designs needed a superman
as pilot. He was required to
crouch in an upright position
and operate four wings at
once by turning windlasses
(revolving cylinders) with
his hands and feet. He also
had to push a piston up and
down with his head. The
plan also featured special
flaps, which opened on the
upstroke to let through air
and ease the pressure, but
closed on the downstroke to
increase the pressure. This
idea was later utilized in
aircraft construction.

Exploring the heavens

T HE BASIC SHAPE OF THE UNIVERSE had been defined by the Greek astronomer Ptolemy back in the 2nd century. His theory stated that the Earth is a static body at the centre of the Universe, and that the planets and the Sun revolve around it. This geocentric, or Earth-centred, view had become a cornerstone of Western thought – especially religion. But the Renaissance provoked a fresh spirit of enquiry. In 1543, the Polish astronomer Nicolaus Copernicus (1473–1543) put forward an amazing new theory: that the Sun is at the centre of the Universe, around which the Earth and other planets revolve. This idea led to a revolution in astronomy.

MARINER'S MODEL
The armillary sphere had been used since Ptolemy's time to teach navigators and others about the arrangement of the heavens. It was a hollow model of the solar system, with the Earth at the centre and metal rings representing the paths of the Sun and the planets.

Metal rings rotate to show the courses of the planets

HEAVENS ABOVE
Thanks to the development of the telescope, the Italian physicist and astronomer Galileo Galilei (1564–1642) was able to observe the night sky in greater detail than anyone before him. He discovered that several moons revolve around Jupiter. This meant that not all heavenly bodies circled the Earth; therefore it could not be at the centre of the Universe. Copernicus' theory was proved correct.

Venetian senators amazed at the view through Galileo's telescope

TRACKING THE PLANETS
From his observatory near Copenhagen, Denmark, astronomer Tycho Brahe (1546–1601) made precise recordings of the movements of the planets. His observations were so accurate that the first complete modern stellar atlas was produced from them.

THE PTOLEMAIC SYSTEM
The Earth sits at the centre of Ptolemy's Universe, circled by the planets and stars. Christian teaching used this system to show that God had designed the Universe for the sole benefit of human beings.

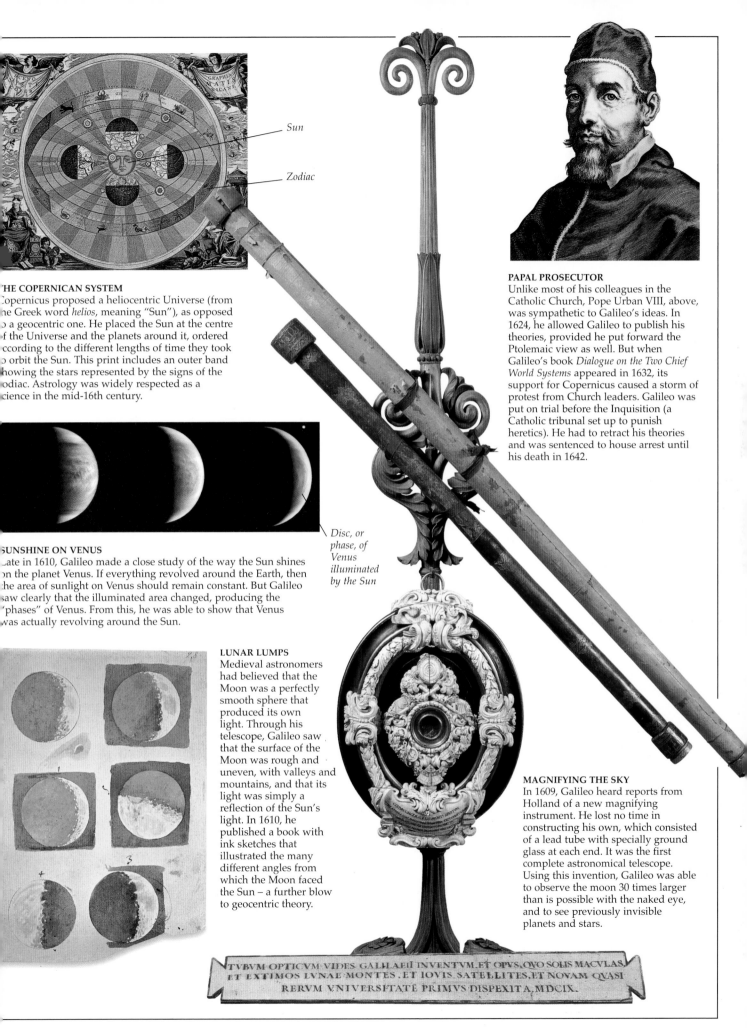

THE COPERNICAN SYSTEM

Copernicus proposed a heliocentric Universe (from the Greek word *helios*, meaning "Sun"), as opposed to a geocentric one. He placed the Sun at the centre of the Universe and the planets around it, ordered according to the different lengths of time they took to orbit the Sun. This print includes an outer band showing the stars represented by the signs of the zodiac. Astrology was widely respected as a science in the mid-16th century.

Sun

Zodiac

SUNSHINE ON VENUS

Late in 1610, Galileo made a close study of the way the Sun shines on the planet Venus. If everything revolved around the Earth, then the area of sunlight on Venus should remain constant. But Galileo saw clearly that the illuminated area changed, producing the "phases" of Venus. From this, he was able to show that Venus was actually revolving around the Sun.

Disc, or phase, of Venus illuminated by the Sun

LUNAR LUMPS

Medieval astronomers had believed that the Moon was a perfectly smooth sphere that produced its own light. Through his telescope, Galileo saw that the surface of the Moon was rough and uneven, with valleys and mountains, and that its light was simply a reflection of the Sun's light. In 1610, he published a book with ink sketches that illustrated the many different angles from which the Moon faced the Sun – a further blow to geocentric theory.

PAPAL PROSECUTOR

Unlike most of his colleagues in the Catholic Church, Pope Urban VIII, above, was sympathetic to Galileo's ideas. In 1624, he allowed Galileo to publish his theories, provided he put forward the Ptolemaic view as well. But when Galileo's book *Dialogue on the Two Chief World Systems* appeared in 1632, its support for Copernicus caused a storm of protest from Church leaders. Galileo was put on trial before the Inquisition (a Catholic tribunal set up to punish heretics). He had to retract his theories and was sentenced to house arrest until his death in 1642.

MAGNIFYING THE SKY

In 1609, Galileo heard reports from Holland of a new magnifying instrument. He lost no time in constructing his own, which consisted of a lead tube with specially ground glass at each end. It was the first complete astronomical telescope. Using this invention, Galileo was able to observe the moon 30 times larger than is possible with the naked eye, and to see previously invisible planets and stars.

TVBVM OPTICVM VIDES GALILAEI INVENTVM,ET OPVS,QVO SOLIS MACVLAS, ET EXTIMOS LVNAE MONTES,ET IOVIS SATELLITES,ET NOVAM QVASI RERVM VNIVERSITATE PRIMVS DISPEXIT A,MDCIX.

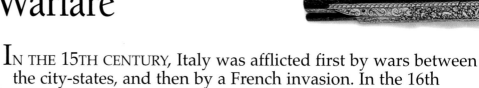

Warfare

IN THE 15TH CENTURY, Italy was afflicted first by wars between the city-states, and then by a French invasion. In the 16th century, wars over religion divided the whole of Europe. The development of firearms and explosives led to a rapid advance in the technology of warfare. The military engineer became an important figure, not simply for designing weapons, but for improving fortifications, building bridges, and even diverting rivers to destroy the enemy. So, when Leonardo moved to Milan in 1482, he wrote to the duke, Lodovico Sforza, and offered his services as an engineer who could design anything from giant catapults to warship.

CANNONIZED
When the French armies invaded Italy in 1494, the Italians were impressed by their advanced weaponry, which included cannons that fired iron balls. In Florence, the Medici later ordered similar cannons to be made. Some were even decorated with cast heads of saints, such as Saint Peter, above.

Shells explode on impact

MORTAR BOMBS
"I have bombardment devices that will hurl rocks as thickly as hailstones, with the smoke causing great terror to the enemy," wrote Leonardo to Lodovico Sforza. His mortar cannon was designed to lob shells in an arc over defensive walls. The shells would then explode, shattering small stones like modern shrapnel.

Screw-jack for raising or lowering elevation

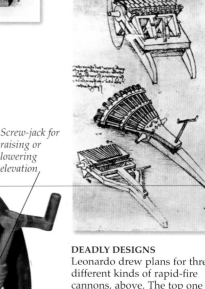

DEADLY DESIGNS
Leonardo drew plans for three different kinds of rapid-fire cannons, above. The top one h all barrels pointing in a single direction, the middle one has splayed barrels, and the botton one has three racks of guns, which could be fired one after another.

Iron-rimmed wheels

Flap gives access for reloading

SPRAYING THE TARGET
None of Leonardo's multi-barrelled guns was built in his lifetime, but this modern model is based on his designs. The eight light cannon could fire iron-tipped bolts over a wide area – a deadly tactic against an advancing body of troops.

Wheel-lock gun

Wheel-lock pistol

Butt could be used as a club

Magazine for storing spare flints

OCK, STOCK, AND BARREL

unpowder had been used for warfare in Europe since the ...th century, but it was only after about 1425 that small ...ms became effective in battle. The wheel-lock gun and ...stol, above, are both from the late 1500s, and are operated ... the same mechanism. They were fired by pulling a ...gger that spun a wheel. The wheel struck sparks from a ...nt or piece of iron pyrites, and the sparks ignited the ...unpowder. Despite their power, such weapons were ...pensive to make and slow to reload.

OWDER FLASK

...oldiers carried flasks filled ...ith gunpowder, which they ...pped out of the spout when ...loading their weapons. The ...asks were made of non-ferrous ...aterials, such as horn, to ...event accidental sparks.

PROUD SOLDIER
Leonardo's drawing of a warrior conveys all the arrogance and cruelty of the *condottieri*, or mercenary soldiers, hired by several of the city-states to fight their battles. By 1509, Venice employed nearly 30,000 of them. In fact, some mercenary bands prolonged wars so that they could continue to receive their wages.

Lion's head, a symbol of Florence

MEDICI SWORD
Swords were still vital weapons in 16th-century warfare, and Milanese ironworkers were famed throughout Europe for the high quality and beauty of their arms and armour. This ornate falchion, or short cutting sword, is engraved with the crest of Cosimo I de' Medici.

Medici coat of arms

Death and disease

Between the 10th and 15th centuries, diseases such as smallpox, dysentery, and typhus arrived in Europe, brought by travellers from other countries. Most virulent of all was the plague, which reached Italy in 1348. Florence, like many other cities, lost more than one third of its population. Further outbreaks of the plague continued throughout the 15th and 16th centuries. Contact with the New World (the Americas) was the probable cause of the introduction of syphilis, which spread across Europe in the 1490s. Treatment of disease was often based on superstition and prayer. Meanwhile, death in childbirth, high infant death rates, and constant warring continued to make Renaissance Europe a dangerous place to live.

SEARING PAIN
The cautery iron was heated until red-hot and applied to wounds and ulcers. It seared the flesh and stopped bleeding, destroying the swellings caused by the plague but not the infection itself.

PRIEST'S PROTECTOR
Priests were often called to bless the sick and dying. To protect themselves from infection, they used a long-handled instrument like this for offering communion bread and wine, and for sprinkling holy water on the patient.

BLOODSUCKERS
Doctors believed that many illnesses could be relieved by draining "poisons" or excess blood from the body – a process known as bloodletting. Some used medicinal leeches to suck out blood.

DUTY TO THE SICK
This manuscript illumination shows an Italian hospital of the 15th century. Care of the sick was considered a religious duty, and wealthy merchants gave money to found hospitals. On a visit to Italy in 1511, Martin Luther noted that "the hospitals are handsomely built and admirably provided with careful attendants". However, treatment was mostly ineffectual, and victims of disease were encouraged to concentrate on the fate of their souls rather than that of their bodies.

CARRYING THE PLAGUE
The plague was first brought to Italy in ships returning from the Black Sea. The virus was carried by a species of flea that lived on black rats and other rodents. Once on dry land, the rats lived in people's homes, and spread the deadly virus to humans.

Plague fleas infested the fur of the rat

CROSSES OF LEAD
Without any cure for the plague, people took preventive measures, which could be cruel as well as sensible. Infected families were boarded up in their houses, patients were isolated in plague hospitals, infected clothing was burned, and bodies were buried in mass graves, or plague pits, well away from the towns. Coffins were scarce, so a simple lead cross was placed on each corpse.

Cautery iron

Communion instrument

Map showing the signs of the zodiac

DEATH TAKES A CHILD
This woodcut shows a child being dragged from its parents by a devil (representing death). Repeated outbreaks of the plague reinforced the medieval belief that illness and early death were punishments from God for human wickedness. Such beliefs were particularly strong in northern Europe.

SYPHILITIC STARS
Syphilis caused sores and pustules to form all over the victim's body. Albrecht Dürer depicted the harrowing consequences of the disease in this woodcut, which also illustrates the power of superstition. The globe above the victim's head displays the year 1484, when the new epidemic was thought to have been caused by the appearance of five planets in the zodiacal sign of the scorpion.

POISONOUS CURE
In 1512, doctors began to use mercury to treat syphilis. They did not realize that mercury is poisonous and can be deadly.

Crib decorated with mythological figures

DEATH AT BIRTH
In Renaissance Europe, between a quarter and a half of all babies died in their first year. With little proper treatment available, common illnesses such as influenza and measles could easily kill vulnerable babies. Children born to poor families were also particularly at risk from malnutrition.

h-century ian baby's crib

A reading public

THE INVENTION OF THE PRINTING PRESS was one of the most dramatic developments to affect the Renaissance world. Printing had first been developed in China, where movable type was used as early as the 11th century. But it was not until the 1450s that the method was adopted in Europe, when the German Johannes Gutenberg (c. 1398–1468) began printing entire books using movable type cast in metal. For the first time, exact copies of books could be produced quickly and cheaply. By about 1500 there were over 1,000 printing workshops in Europe, mostly in Germany and Italy.

IN THE WORKSHOP
The bustle of a printing office was very different from the quiet of a medieval scribe's desk. This 16th-century picture shows everyone hard at work. The compositor sets type, the printers operate the press, and the proofreader checks a printed page for errors. Only the dog is asleep.

ITALIAN ITALICS
German printers used thick, Gothic type that resembled that of old manuscripts. Italian printers cast smaller types, such as *italic*, shown above, and roman. With these typefaces, more words could fit on a page, so fewer pages were needed, and books became smaller and cheaper

GUTENBERG BIBLE
Gutenberg was a skilled craftsman. He built his printing press by applying the principle of the press used to crush grapes for wine, and he engraved metal punches for moulding the type in relief. His workshop could print about 300 sheets each day. In 1455, Gutenberg produced his first complete printed book – the Bible. His edition, known as the Gutenberg Bible, contained over 1,200 pages in two volumes, and it probably took several years to set and print.

Printed books continued to be decorated by hand

PROUD PRINTER
Johannes Gutenberg displays a newly printed sheet in his workshop.

Pieces of type specially shaped to fit neatly together

TYPESETTING
Each character, or letter, was cast (in mirror image) on a separate piece of type. The compositor picked out the type and set it in order on a "stick" (left). Spaces between words o blocks of text were filled with blank "leading". The movable grip on the le fixed the line length.

Grip

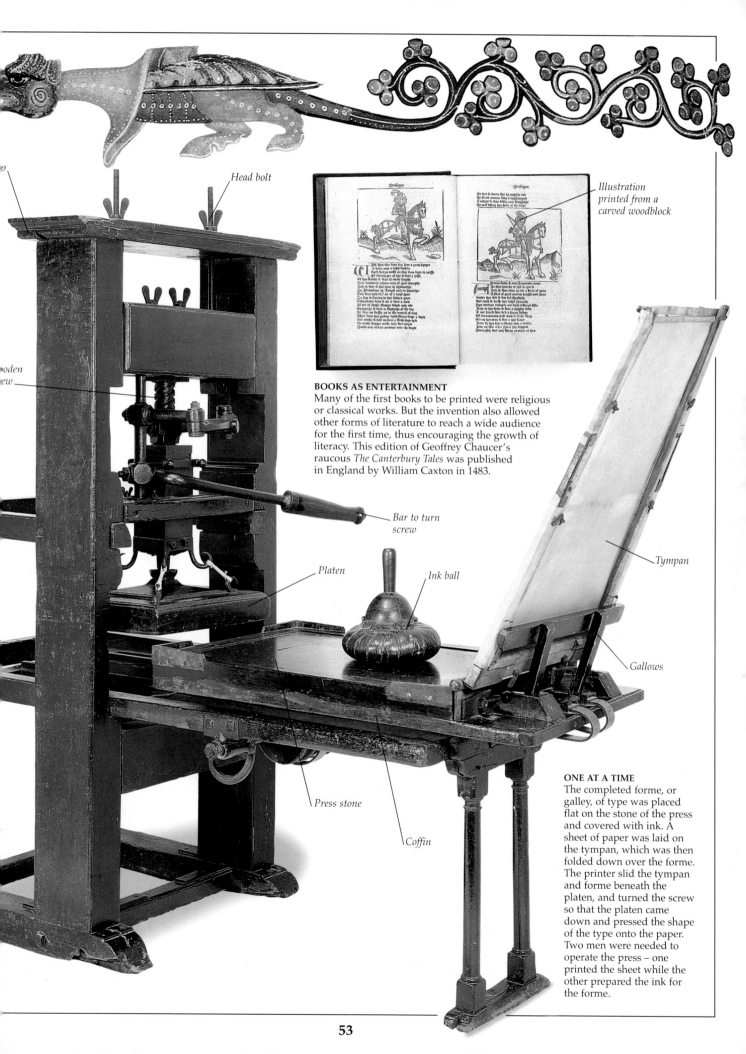

Head bolt

Illustration printed from a carved woodblock

BOOKS AS ENTERTAINMENT
Many of the first books to be printed were religious or classical works. But the invention also allowed other forms of literature to reach a wide audience for the first time, thus encouraging the growth of literacy. This edition of Geoffrey Chaucer's raucous *The Canterbury Tales* was published in England by William Caxton in 1483.

Wooden screw

Bar to turn screw

Platen

Ink ball

Tympan

Press stone

Gallows

Coffin

ONE AT A TIME
The completed forme, or galley, of type was placed flat on the stone of the press and covered with ink. A sheet of paper was laid on the tympan, which was then folded down over the forme. The printer slid the tympan and forme beneath the platen, and turned the screw so that the platen came down and pressed the shape of the type onto the paper. Two men were needed to operate the press – one printed the sheet while the other prepared the ink for the forme.

Music and leisure

WORKING LIFE WAS HARD for most people in Renaissance Europe, and there was little money or time to spend on entertainment. But even the poorest could enjoy the regular religious feast days, which meant a day's holiday from work, free food, and the excitement of processions, horse races, and mock battles. The people could also go to the great churches to hear the pure, sensuous new music for the Mass. The wealthy, of course, could afford far grander amusements, including many outdoor sports, especially hunting.

COMPOSER FOR THE CHURCH
Giovanni Pierluigi da Palestrina (c. 1525–94) composed more than 100 settings of the Mass and many simpler works for unaccompanied voices. His choral compositions were intricate and sumptuous, while the words were always clear and intelligible.

NOTES ON THE PAGE
The invention of printing had a huge impact on music. For the first time, scores could be copied accurately and quickly, and they were sold widely throughout Europe. The first music printed from movable type was published by Ottaviano Petrucci in Venice in 1501. He went on to produce over 59 volumes, from polyphony to lute music, shown above.

LEONARDO'S MUS[IC]
Leonardo had a fine singing voice and was a skilled player of the lira da braccia (left). He made his own lyre from silver, which was said to have a more resonant and beautiful sound than a conventional wooden lyre. His notebooks also contain studies for many other instruments, including mechanical drums and wind instruments with keyboards. For Leonardo, music was "the representati[on] of invisible things", and the sister of painting.

An angel plays heavenly music on the lute

Music

Renaissance music was written mainly for voices. The great choirs of the cathedrals sang settings of the liturgy (religious services) or oratorios (religious stories set to music). The style was polyphonic, which means it contained several melodies that were sung simultaneously. Outside the Church, the most popular form of music was the madrigal, which was usually romantic poetry with parts for several voices.

Hunting

Hunting had been a popular pastime for the wealthy and nobility since the Middle Ages, and its popularity continued in Renaissance times. Hunting parties could be enormous – entire courts might take part – and could last for several weeks. It was also highly energetic; it was said that Henry VIII of England could wear out eight horses in a single day's hunting.

HAWK HOOD
Birds and small animals were hunted with falcons. The falconer placed a hood, such as this one, over the falcon's head in order to "hoodwink" it into thinking it was night, so the bird would remain calm. When the hunter spotted suitable game, he removed the hood and released his hawk.

Decorative feather plume

HUNTING HORN
The huntsman organized the hunt and led the hounds. He blew a horn to signal that game was sighted, or to indicate the direction in which it was headed. Some hunting horns were very ornate, such as this one made of buffalo horn and gilded bronze.

A WOMAN'S WEAPON
This unusual crossbow was made especially for a woman. Designed for shooting birds, it used clay balls instead of arrows. Although most hunters were men, some women, including Queen Elizabeth I of England (1533–1603), also enjoyed the sport.

Trigger for releasing bowstring

Festivals

Leisure time was associated not with weekends, as it is now, but with public holidays (holy days), which were much more numerous than they are today. Holidays were festival days, celebrated with plays, games, and processions.

THE OMMEGANCK PROCESSION
Royal processions were also occasions for festivals. In 1615, the townsfolk of Brussels, Belgium, were treated to a particularly spectacular triumphal procession celebrating the entry of the Regent Isabella. It featured more than a dozen floats carrying people dressed as symbolic and mythical figures.

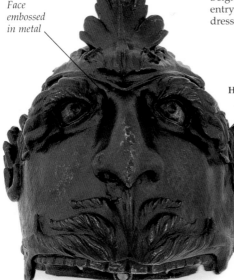

Face embossed in metal

HELMETS ON PARADE
This Italian casque, or open helmet, was made in about 1530, especially for use in parades. Such helmets were worn for Carnival, the wildest of all Italian festivals, celebrated during the period preceding Lent. In addition to parades, it included huge banquets, organized races, and tournaments.

RENAISSANCE REVISITED
Italians still re-enact the parades of medieval and Renaissance times. At this festival in Oristano, Sardinia, a procession of drummers, trumpeters, and knights parades through the city. Held each February, the festival is thought to bring a prosperous year.

The Renaissance in the north

"IMMORTAL GOD, what a world I see dawning!", wrote the Dutch humanist Erasmus in 1517. Like other northern scholars and scientists, he was thrilled by the new horizons opened up by the Renaissance in Italy. Artists too, such as Dürer and Holbein, were inspired by Italian masters. Many travelled to Italy to study the rediscovered classical texts, absorb new ideas, and acquire new techniques. At the same time, patrons such as François I of France encouraged Italian artists, and promoted the use of printed books and manuscripts.

HONEST ESSAYIST
"I myself am the subject of my book," admitted Miche de Montaigne (1533–92) in the introduction to his essays, written in a seclud tower in France. No writer before had ever revealed himself so honestly or humanely. Montaigne's thoughts on friendship, parenthood, and other personal matters exemplify the spirit of Renaissance humani

Tiny, distant figures skate on the ice

FROZEN LANDSCAPE
The Flemish artist Pieter Brueghel the Elder (c. 1525–69) travelled from Flanders to Italy, although he was more inspired by the Alps than by Italian art. His detailed landscapes, such as this one, *Hunters in the Snow* (1565), show country people in their natural environment. His work illustrates the lively realism of much northern painting.

IDEAL BEAUTY
Painted by Albrecht Dürer in 1507, these twin pictures of Adam and Eve are the first idealized nudes in German art. They embody the classical quest for ideal beauty that was common to Italian art. Dürer was responsible for bringing many Italian Renaissance ideas to northern Europe.

JOURNEY TO THE UNDERWORLD
Flemish painter Joachim Patinir (c. 1480–1525) has been referred to as the first Western artist known to have specialized in landscape painting. The subject of *Crossing the River Styx* is a mythological one – the souls of the dead are being rowed across the river to the Underworld by Charon, the ferryman. Patinir combined a strong sense of fantasy with a brilliant use of light and shade and detailed observation.

DUTCH SCHOLAR

Desiderius Erasmus (1466–1536) travelled widely throughout Europe. A leading humanist scholar of the northern Renaissance, he succeeded in popularizing a range of classical texts for ordinary readers. He also attacked corruption in the Catholic Church, although he did not support the Protestant movement. This portrait was painted by his friend, the German artist Hans Holbein (1497–1543), who is famous for his realistic depictions of physical features.

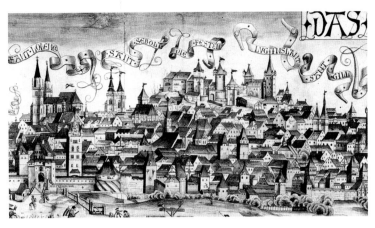

NUREMBERG, CITY OF CULTURE

By the mid-16th century, Nuremberg, in present-day southern Germany, had become a prosperous trading and cultural centre. The city was home to artists such as Dürer, and it boasted one of the first printing presses and a library containing 4,000 volumes. Printmakers, mapmakers, and astronomers, as well as artists and scholars, were attracted to Nuremberg by wealthy patrons.

A candle burning in a daylit room was traditional for newlyweds

Dog symbolizes obedience

GARGANTUAN SUCCESS

French writer François Rabelais (c. 1490–1553) ridiculed old-fashioned, formal ways of teaching compared to the new humanism in his boisterous, comic novels *Pantagruel* (1532) and *Gargantua* (1534). They were massive bestsellers throughout Europe, although they were banned in France for some time.

DOMESTIC DETAILS

Artists in the Netherlands pioneered their own oil-painting techniques in the early 15th century, creating a naturalistic style that influenced even Italian painters. Jan van Eyck (c. 1390–1441) painted this double portrait *The Arnolfini Marriage* (1434) in astonishingly precise detail. The painting is believed to celebrate the wedding of an Italian merchant, Giovanni Arnolfini, and many of its details refer to the sacred union of marriage.

GLITTERING GLASS

The English architect Robert Smythson was greatly influenced by Italian architectural ideas. His design for Hardwick Hall (completed 1597) in Derbyshire, England, included so many windows that it was described as "more glass than wall".

The Renaissance legacy

As RENAISSANCE HUMANISM spread across Europe during the 16th century, it gave people the freedom to look at the world in fresh ways, to express individual thoughts, and to question traditional views. And the achievements of the Renaissance went on to inspire and influence the Western world in the following century. Painters and sculptors were no longer regarded as craftsmen but as fine artists. Writers such as Shakespeare could use language with a new exuberance and beauty. Scientists such as Newton could examine how the Universe functioned. The philosophers Blaise Pascal (1623–62) and René Descartes (1596–1650) could look rationally at the relationship between human beings and God.

PAINTING A LIFE
Over 40 years, the great Dutch painter Rembrandt van Rijn (1606–69) produced a series of self-portraits. These made an unflinchingly honest record of the artist's life, from youthful success, through loss and bankruptcy, to old age. The series embodies the humanist theme that each person's experience is unique, and tells an individual story.

Rembrandt aged 23

Rembrandt aged 55

Cambridge University

A NEW LITERATURE
The Spanish writer Miguel de Cervantes (1547–1616) created two immortal comic characters, Don Quixote and his servant Sancho Panza. The best-selling adventures of Don Quixote not only made fun of Renaissance chivalry, but were also the model for a new kind of anti-heroic fiction.

CENTRE OF LEARNING
Many Renaissance statesmen encouraged the spread of humanist learning. The famous Dutch scholar Erasmus was, for a time, professor of Greek at Cambridge University in England, which became a centre of humanist teaching.

Don Quixote's scrawny old horse, Rozinante

THE THEATRE
William Shakespeare (1564–1616) forged a fresh and dynamic kind of verse drama, often using earlier plays and romances as his sources. Many of his plays, such as *The Merchant of Venice* and *Romeo and Juliet*, were set in Renaissance Italy. Much of Shakespeare's greatest work was first performed at the Globe in London, an open-air theatre built in 1599. This model shows the stage and surrounding galleries. In 1997, a working reconstruction of Shakespeare's Globe was completed near the original site.

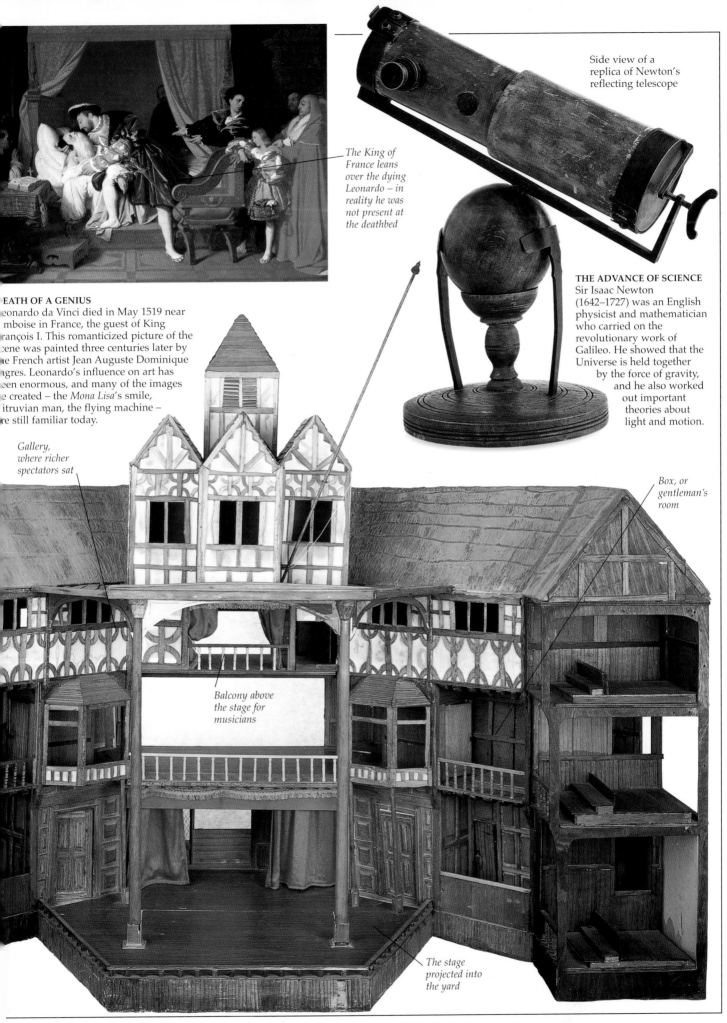

Side view of a replica of Newton's reflecting telescope

The King of France leans over the dying Leonardo – in reality he was not present at the deathbed

DEATH OF A GENIUS

Leonardo da Vinci died in May 1519 near Amboise in France, the guest of King François I. This romanticized picture of the scene was painted three centuries later by the French artist Jean Auguste Dominique Ingres. Leonardo's influence on art has been enormous, and many of the images he created – the *Mona Lisa*'s smile, Vitruvian man, the flying machine – are still familiar today.

THE ADVANCE OF SCIENCE

Sir Isaac Newton (1642–1727) was an English physicist and mathematician who carried on the revolutionary work of Galileo. He showed that the Universe is held together by the force of gravity, and he also worked out important theories about light and motion.

Gallery, where richer spectators sat

Box, or gentleman's room

Balcony above the stage for musicians

The stage projected into the yard

Did you know?

Leonardo wrote in Italian, using a type of shorthand that he invented himself. He also used "mirror" writing – writing each line from right to left and reversing every letter.

Sample of Leonardo's "mirror" writing

Although Leonardo wrote with his left hand, he used both his left and right hand to draw and paint.

Leonardo signed his works Leonardo or *Io, Leonardo* (I, Leonardo).

Leonardo was a practical person. In one of his notebooks, he breaks off writing his thoughts on geometry "... because the soup is getting cold."

Leonardo's early drawings include systems of hydraulics and mechanisms for breathing underwater, as well as an automated cart known as Leonardo's automobile.

Andrea del Verrocchio (1435–88) was the master of the workshop where Leonardo was apprenticed. It has been suggested that Leonardo may have posed for Verrocchio's bronze sculpture of *David*.

The Florentine artist Paolo Uccello (1397–1475) was so enamoured with the new science of perspective, according to art historian Vasari, that he stayed up all night searching for vanishing points.

Michelangelo painted all the frescoes on the ceiling of the Sistine Chapel himself, dismissing his helpers because he considered their work to be inferior.

Apothecaries were the main suppliers of pigments (colours in powdered form from natural earths, minerals, plants, or animals stuffs) and worked closely with painters. In Florence, apothecaries and painters belonged to the same guild, the Guild of St Luke, along with spice merchants and doctors.

Leonardo was reportedly a vegetarian who loved animals so much that he is said to have bought caged birds at markets so he could set them free.

Leonardo saw the human body as the ultimate machine. He often used its components to solve intricate mechanical problems, basing the wiring of a music keyboard on the tendons in a hand, and designing a musical recorder based on the upper larynx.

A bird flies free

Leonardo's unfinished painting *St Jerome* (c. 1480) was discovered in two parts. The lower part formed the cover of a chest, and the saint's head was found in the shop of a shoemaker, where it was being used to cover a stool.

The name of the *Codex Atlanticus*, a collection of Leonardo's writings, refers to its large, atlas-sized format – the codex is about 60 cm (2 ft) tall.

More than 5,000 pages of notes and drawings by Leonardo survive. Experts now think that thousands more did exist but are now lost. In 1967, 700 pages of handwritten notes were discovered by chance in Madrid's National Library.

David by Andrea del Verrocchio

When painting *The Last Supper*, Leonardo spent a lot of time wandering through the jails of Milan looking for a suitable model for Judas.

Napoleon loved the *Mona Lisa* so much that he took it from the Louvre, in Paris, and hung it in his bedroom.

Leonardo's *Mona Lisa* was stolen from the Louvre in 1911. The painting was found two years later in the false bottom of a trunk in Florence. While the painting was missing, six forgeries turned up in the USA, each one selling for a high price.

In 1994, one of Leonardo's notebooks, the *Codex Leicester*, was bought by Bill Gates, chairman of the Microsoft Corporation, for US$30 million.

In 2001, Leonardo's drawing *Horse and Rider* (dated 1481–82) fetched £8,143,750 at an auction at Christie's in London. It was bought by an anonymous telephone bidder, and is the only one of Leonardo's sketches still privately owned.

When it was first published in 2003, *The Da Vinci Code* – which centres around Leonardo's painting of *The Last Supper* – was only moderately successful. Two years later, 25 million books in 44 languages had been printed.

Leonardo often planned great paintings with many drawings and sketches but left the projects unfinished. Only 17 of Leonardo's paintings survive.

In 2005, experts at London's National Gallery used infrared reflectography to see through layers of paint and discovered earlier drawings beneath the surface of Leonardo's *The Virgin of the Rocks*.

Author Dan Brown with copies of his bestseller *The Da Vinci Code*

QUESTIONS AND ANSWERS

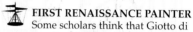

Detail of the *Mona Lisa*

Q Why does the *Mona Lisa* appear to have no eyebrows?

A The most likely explanation is that Leonardo did put in eyebrows as a final touch when the paint on the face was dry. However, the first time it was cleaned (perhaps in the 17th century), the restorer used the wrong solvent and the eyebrows dissolved and were removed forever.

Q Why did Leonardo use "mirror" writing in his notebooks?

A No one knows for sure. As he was left-handed, Leonardo may have found writing from right to left less messy – he would not have smudged the ink with his hand as he wrote. Perhaps he was trying to make it harder for others to read his ideas and steal them. He may even have been trying to hide his writings from the Roman Catholic Church, whose teachings would not have agreed with his scientific ideas and discoveries.

Giotto's 13th-century fresco cycle from the Basilica of San Francesco, Assisi

Q Why are there two versions of Leonardo's painting *The Virgin of the Rocks*?

A Even historians are divided on this. The first version of the painting was commissioned by the Confraternity of the Immaculate Conception in San Francesco, Milan, but for some reason did not satisfy its patrons. It was probably sold in the 1490s to a private client, and now hangs in the Louvre in Paris. Leonardo began a second version of the painting in about 1493, probably to fulfil his contract. This painting, which now hangs in the National Gallery in London, was accepted by the Confraternity.

Q How did the Medici family help to promote the arts in Florence?

A Rulers from the rich and powerful Medici family, such as Cosimo the Elder (1389–1464) and his grandson Lorenzo (1449–92), spent a great part of their wealth cultivating literature and the arts. Cosimo amassed the largest library in Europe, and commissioned artists such as Lorenzo Ghiberti, Filippo Brunelleschi, and Fra Angelico. Lorenzo the Magnificent was patron of artists such as Sandro Botticelli, Domenico Ghirlandaio, Filippino Lippi, Andrea del Verrocchio, and Michelangelo. However, none of the Medici family ever hired Leonardo or bought any of his paintings.

Medici family crest

Q Why did Leonardo's *The Last Supper* need to be restored?

A *The Last Supper* started to deteriorate during Leonardo's lifetime because the experimental painting methods used did not last, and within 50 years the paint was barely visible. There have been several restorations and re-paintings. The most recent, completed in 1999, took 20 years.

Record Breakers

FIRST RENAISSANCE PAINTER
Some scholars think that Giotto di Bondone (c. 1267–1337) was the first great Renaissance painter. Others say he was an isolated phenomenon and that the true Renaissance did not begin until the explosion of learning in Florence in the 1400s.

FIRST RENAISSANCE BUILDING
The Hospital of the Innocents, Florence, was designed and built by architect Filippo Brunelleschi. Begun in 1419, it is often referred to as the first Renaissance building.

FIRST BOOK PRINTED IN EUROPE
The Gutenberg Bible was printed by moveable type (letters cast in metal) by German Johann Gutenberg in 1455. It is estimated that he printed 180 copies – 145 on paper and the rest on vellum, a fine parchment prepared from calfskin.

FIRST SIGNED WORK BY LEONARDO
A drawing dated 5 August, 1473 (the feast day of the Virgin of the Snows in Tuscany) is Leonardo's first signed work. It is now held in the Uffizi Gallery, in Florence.

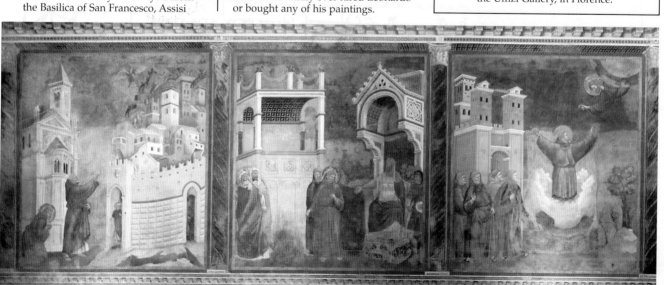

Timeline of the Renaissance

THE RENAISSANCE WAS A PERIOD in the history of western Europe that began in the early 14th century and lasted almost to the end of the 16th century. It was marked by a great explosion of learning and a spirit of rebirth in art, but it was also marred by wars and the devastating spread of the Black Death, a plague that reduced the population by almost one-third. This timeline looks at events which, despite the setbacks, defined this period as one of the great ages of human cultural achievement.

1302–10 Giovanni Pisano (c. 1250–1314) sculpts the pulpit of Pisa Cathedral.

c. 1305 Giotto di Bondone (c. 1267–1337) paints the walls of the Arena Chapel in Padua.

1308 Dante Alighieri (1265–1321) begins his poem, *The Divine Comedy*.

1413–16 The Limbourg brothers illustrate a medieval book of hours known as *Les Très Riches Heures du Duc de Berry*.

1420–36 Filippo Brunelleschi (1377–1446) builds the dome of Florence Cathedral.

1424–27/8 Masaccio (1401–28) and Masolino (active 1423–47) are commissioned to paint the frescoes in the Brancacci Chapel, Santa Maria del Carmine, Florence.

Albrecht Dürer's master engraving *Knight, Death, and the Devil* (1513)

1435 Donatello's (1386–1466) bronze statue of *David* is completed.

1436 Brunelleschi designs the Church of Santo Spirito, Florence. Work does not begin until 1444. Leon Battista Alberti (1404–72) translates into Italian his Latin treatise on painting, *De Pictura*.

1438–1445 Fra Angelico (c. 1400–55) paints scenes from the life of Christ in San Marco Monastery, Florence.

1450 Francesco Sforza (1401–66) becomes Duke of Milan. The Vatican Library is founded in Rome.

1452 Leonardo is born, at Anchiano, near Vinci. Ghiberti completes the bronze East doors for Florence Cathedral.

1453 Hundred Years War ends. Turks capture Constantinople, marking the collapse of the Byzantine Empire.

1455 Johannes Gutenberg (c. 1398–1468) prints the Bible.

1456 Alberti is commissioned to complete the facade on the church of Santa Maria Novella in Florence.

1462 Founding of the Platonic Academy in Florence.

1466 Leonardo moves to Florence.

1469 Leonardo starts his training in the workshop of painter and sculptor Andrea del Verrocchio (1435–88). Lorenzo de' Medici (1449–92) becomes head of the Medici family.

1472 Leonardo finishes his apprenticeship and is entered as an independent master in the Guild of St Luke.

1481–82 Leonardo paints *The Adoration of the Magi*.

1482 Sandro Botticelli (1445–1510) paints *La Primavera*.

Portrait of Dante standing before Florence by Domenico di Michelino (1417–91)

1337 Beginning of the Hundred Years War between France and England.

1348 The plague, known as the Black Death, arrives in Europe via the Italian port of Genoa.

1353 Publication of the *Decameron*, a collection of 100 short stories, told by Giovanni Boccaccio (1313–75).

1364 Charles V (1338–80) becomes king of France.

c. 1424 The Doge's Palace in Venice is completed after 15 years.

1425 Lorenzo Ghiberti (1378–1455) finishes the North doors of Florence Cathedral and is commissioned to make a second set of doors for the East side.

1434 Italian merchant prince Cosimo de' Medici (1389–1464), head of the Medici family, becomes virtual ruler of Florence. Flemish artist Jan Van Eyck (c. 1390–1441) paints *The Arnolfini Marriage*.

Raphael's fresco *The School of Athens* (1509–11)

1482–99 Leonardo works for the Duke of Milan, Ludovico Sforza (c.1451–1508).

c. 1483 Leonardo completes *The Virgin of the Rocks* (Louvre version). William Caxton (1422–91) publishes second edition of Chaucer's (c. 1343–1400) *Canterbury Tales*.

1484 Publication of Marsilio Ficino's (1433–99) translations of the writings of the Greek philosopher, Plato.

1485 Publication of Alberti's *De Re Aedificatoria*, his treatise on architecture. Botticelli paints *The Birth of Venus*.

1490 Leonardo draws the *Vitruvian Man*, complete with accompanying notes.

1492 Explorer Christopher Columbus (1451–1506) reaches the "New World".

1494 Political wars in Italy. German engraver Albrecht Dürer (1471–1528) makes his first trip to Italy.

1495 Aldus Manutius (1449–1515) establishes the Aldine Press in Venice to print classical Greek texts.

1495–97/8 Leonardo paints *The Last Supper*.

1498 Explorer Vasco da Gama (1469–1524) sails round the Cape of Good Hope and reaches India.

1499 The French invade Milan, driving out Duke Ludovico Sforza.

1500 Leonardo returns to Florence and later enters the service of Cesare Borgia as military adviser and engineer. Leonardo paints *The Virgin and Child with Saint Anne*.

1501–04 Michelangelo Buonarroti (1475–1564) sculpts *David*.

c. 1503–06 Leonardo paints the *Mona Lisa*.

1504 Leonardo and Michelangelo are commissioned to produce murals for the Palazzo Vecchio in Florence.

1505 Exhibition of cartoons by Leonardo and Michelangelo in Florence.

1506 Construction begins on the Basilica of St Peter's church in Rome.

c. 1508 Leonardo returns to Milan and completes *The Virgin of the Rocks* (London National Gallery version). Architect Andrea Palladio born in Padua.

1508–12 Michelangelo paints the ceiling of the Sistine Chapel in Rome.

1509–11 Raphael (Raffaello Sanzio, 1483–1520) paints *The School of Athens*.

Facade of Doge's Palace, Venice

1513 Giovanni de' Medici (1475–1521) becomes pope, adopting the name Leo X.

1513–14 Dürer completes *St Jerome in his Study* and *Knight, Death, and the Devil*.

1513–16 Leonardo travels to Rome to work for Pope Leo X.

1516 Leonardo is hired by Francis I, King of France.

1517 Martin Luther (1483–1546), leader of the Protestant Reformation, nails his Ninety-five Theses to the church door at Wittenberg Castle, Germany.

1519 Death of Leonardo, near Amboise in France, at the age of 67.

1520–23 Tiziano Vecellio (c.1488–1576), known as Titian, paints *Bacchus and Ariadne*.

1534 Martin Luther's bible is published. Henry VIII becomes head of the Church of England, breaking with Rome.

1537 Florentine architect Jacopo Sansovino (c.1486–1570) designs the great library in Venice.

1538 Titian paints *Venus of Urbino*.

1543 Nicolaus Copernicus (1473–1543) publishes his opinion that the Earth moves around the Sun. Belgian anatomist Andreas Vesalius (1514–64) publishes the first accurate descriptions of the human body.

1550 Publication of the first edition of Giorgio Vasari's *Lives of the Most Excellent Painters, Sculptors, and Architects*, which includes the first biography of Leonardo.

1550–58 The Boboli Gardens in Florence are planted by the Medici family.

1589 Galileo Galilei (1564–1642) becomes professor of mathematics at Pisa University.

Find out more

THERE ARE MANY EXCELLENT books written about Leonardo, and a wealth of information about him can be discovered on-line. Although you can view Leonardo's paintings on the internet, nothing is better than seeing them first-hand.

The Places to Visit box lists some of the galleries around the world where Leonardo's works are on display, along with those by other Renaissance masters. If you have the chance, a trip to Florence is the best way to see some amazing Renaissance architecture, including Brunelleschi's cathedral dome, and Alberti's facade of the church of Santa Maria Novella.

CODEX ATLANTICUS
It is always worth looking out for touring exhibitions about the Renaissance or Leonardo and his work. For example, an exhibition on the *Codex Atlanticus* (a collection of more than 1,000 sheets of Leonardo's scientific and technical drawings) went on tour in Europe in late 2005, followed by the USA and Japan in 2007.

SEE THE *MONA LISA*
Each year, millions of people visit the Musée du Louvre in Paris to see Leonardo's famous painting, the *Mona Lisa*. The painting is kept behind bullet-proof glass to protect it from damage or theft. People remain fascinated with the *Mona Lisa*'s mysterious smile and continue to wonder who she was. One theory, put forward after studying X-rays of the painting, suggests that the *Mona Lisa* could be a self-portrait of Leonardo.

The Delphic Sibyl, *part of Michelangelo's great fresco in the Sistine Chapel (c. 1509)*

SISTINE CHAPEL
At the Sistine Chapel in Rome, visitors can see recently restored wall paintings by Pietro Perugino, Sandro Botticelli, and Domenico Ghirlandaio, as well as Michelangelo's famous ceiling frescoes depicting scenes from the stages of creation. Restoration work, which took 20 years, was completed in 1999 and has brought back to life colours hidden for hundreds of years by soot and grime.

USEFUL WEBSITES

- To see on-line paintings by Leonardo:
www.ibiblio.org/wm/paint/auth/vinci
- For details of an exhibition on Leonardo held at the Museum of Science, Boston, USA. Website includes a multimedia zone where you can explore perspective, vanishing points, and sfumato:
www.mos.org/leonardo
- To take a virtual tour around the Vatican Museum:
mv.vatican.va
- To see exhibits at the Leonardo Museum in Vinci, including Leonardo's artwork and scale models of his inventions:
www.leonet.it/comuni/vincimus
- Dan Brown's official website, including answers to frequently asked questions about his novel, *The Da Vinci Code*:
www.danbrown.com

VISIT A MUSEUM

You can see a variety of artefacts from the Renaissance at museums, such as the the Victoria and Albert Museum (V&A) in London. From late 2006 until early 2007, the museum presents an exhibition on the homes of Renaissance Italy, recreating the main rooms in an Italian palazzo. There is also an exhibition on the work of Leonardo, displaying a selection of his notebooks as well as models of some of his inventions.

An Italian majolica plate from a display of Renaissance items at the V&A, London

SEE THE ROSSLYN CHAPEL

The Rosslyn Chapel in the village of Roslin, near Edinburgh, features in one of the closing scenes of Dan Brown's novel, *The Da Vinci Code*. The number of people visiting the chapel has greatly increased following the publication of the book. You can find out more about the chapel on its website (www.rosslynchapel.org.uk), which gets around 30,000 hits a week.

The 1-km (2/3-mile) long Vasari corridor connects the Palazzo Vecchio to the Palazzo Pitti.

UFFIZI GALLERY

The Uffizi Gallery in Florence contains a huge collection of Renaissance paintings, including works by Leonardo, Giotto, Botticelli, and Michelangelo. On the top floor of the gallery, visitors can walk along the corridor built by Giorgio Vasari in 1565 to connect the Medici palaces so the family could stroll between them without an escort. The corridor now contains a famous collection of artists' self-portraits.

Places to visit

Here are some of the galleries where you can see Leonardo's paintings as well as works by other Renaissance masters.

ALTE PINAKOTHEK, MUNICH
- Leonardo's *Virgin and Child with a Vase of Flowers* (c. 1478)
- Dürer's *The Four Apostles* (1526) and *Self-portrait in a Fur Coat* (1500s)

CZARTORYSKI MUSEUM, CRACOW
- Leonardo's *The Lady with an Ermine* (1482–85)

THE HERMITAGE, ST PETERSBURG
- Leonardo's *Benois Madonna* (c. 1478) and *The Litta Madonna* (c. 1490–91)
- Titian's *Saint Sebastian* (c. 1570) and *Danae* (c. 1554)

MUSÉE DU LOUVRE, PARIS
- Leonardo's *Mona Lisa* (1503–06), *The Virgin of the Rocks* (1483), and *The Virgin and Child with Saint Anne* (1510)
- Raphael's *Baldassacre Castiglione* (c. 1516)
- Titian's *Man with a Glove* (c. 1523)

NATIONAL GALLERY, LONDON
- Leonardo's *The Virgin of the Rocks* (c. 1508)
- Botticellli's *Venus and Mars* (c. 1485)
- Raphael's *The Ansidei Madonna* (c. 1505)
- Titian's *Bacchus and Ariadne* (1520–23)
- Van Eyck's *The Arnolfini Marriage* (1434)

NATIONAL GALLERY OF ART, WASHINGTON, D.C.
- Leonardo's *Ginevra de Benci* (c. 1475)
- Raphael's *St George Fighting the Dragon* (1504–06) and *Small Cowper Madonna,* (c. 1505)

UFFIZI GALLERY, FLORENCE
- Leonardo's *Annunciation* (1472–5) and *Adoration of the Magi* (1481–)
- Botticelli's *Birth of Venus* (1485) and *La Primavera* (1482)
- Fillippino Lippi's *Madonna and Child* (1485-90)
- Michelangelo's *Holy Family* (1505-07)
- Titian's *Venus of Urbino* (1538)

VATICAN MUSEUM, ROME
- Leonardo's *St Jerome* (1481)
- Raphael's *The School of Athens* (1483–1520)
- Michelangelo's *The Creation of Man* (1508–12)

Leonardo's *The Litta Madonna*

Glossary

ALTARPIECE A religious work of art placed above and behind the altar table.

ANNUNCIATION The announcement by the archangel Gabriel to the Virgin Mary that she would be the mother of Jesus Christ. (Bible reference Luke 1: 26–28.)

APPRENTICE A young person learning an art or craft from a skilled master. An apprenticeship was the main way of entering a trade in medieval Europe.

APPRENTICESHIP A length of time in which an apprentice is legally bound to work for a master of a particular craft.

ARCHANGEL GABRIEL The messenger of god, often depicted in art as the angel of the Annunciation. (*see also* ANNUNCIATION)

ATTRIBUTION The assignment of a work of art to a particular artist, when authorship of that work is not certain.

BACKGROUND An area of a picture that appears farthest from the viewer.

BOLE Soft, fine clay used to coat a panel before it is gilded. The clay is mixed with whisked egg white, then applied with a brush. Bole is usually orange or red, but can be pale pink, grey, or green. Its colour affects the appearance of the gold leaf placed over it.

BYZANTINE A style of art and architecture which developed in the Byzantine Empire and later spread to Italy.

CANVAS Strong woven cloth used for painting, traditionally made of linen or hemp that is stretched over a frame then coated with a ground such as gesso. Canvas became more common for paintings from 1450. (*see also* GESSO, GROUND)

CARTOON A full-scale preparatory drawing on heavy paper or thin card, from the Italian *cartone*, meaning "cardboard". (*see also* FRESCO)

CHIAROSCURO An Italian word meaning "light" (*chiaro*) and "dark" (*oscuro*), referring to the use of light and shade in a painting to suggest three-dimensional form.

CONDOTTIERE A mercenary soldier.

CRISTALLO A clear glass made by Venetian craftsmen in the 1400s leading to the manufacture of silvered mirrors.

DIPTYCH A painting made up of two panels, usually hinged together.

EGG TEMPERA A technique in which powdered colour in water is bound in a medium of egg rather than oil. The egg binds the paint particles together. As the proteins in the egg harden, the colours form a tough skin and a velvety sheen.

Detail from a fresco at the Villa Farnesina, Rome

ENGRAVING A way of cutting a design into a material, usually metal, with a sharp tool called a graver.

ERMINE A small mammal whose fur was used for soft-hair paint brushes. Harder brushes were made with pig bristles.

Altarpiece by Titian of the *Assumption of the Virgin* in Santa Maria Gloriosa dei Frari, Venice

FLORIN A small gold coin stamped with the emblem of the city of Florence – the lily. By 1450, the florin had become the most important currency in Europe.

FOCAL POINT The part of a composition on which the viewer's attention is centred. In Leonardo's *The Last Supper*, the focal point is the figure of Christ.

FOREGROUND An area of a picture that appears closest to the viewer.

FORESHORTENING A way of drawing an object to make it look closer than it really is. (*see also* PICTURE PLANE, PERSPECTIVE)

FRESCO A technique in which paint is applied rapidly onto wet plaster so that the colours penetrate the plaster and set. From the Italian word for "fresh".

GESSO Thin covering made from white chalk, warm glue, and water brushed onto a surface, such as wood, to prepare it for painting or gilding with gold leaf. (*see also* GOLD LEAF)

GILDING Applying gold leaf.

GOLD LEAF Wafer-thin sheets of gold foil used for decoration. The gold is burnished to make it gleam.

GOTHIC A style of art and architecture in northern Europe, dating from the 12th to the 16th century. The term Gothic was invented by Renaissance Italians. It comes from "Goths" – the name of the Germanic tribes who helped destroy the Roman Empire.

GROUND Preparatory surface of primer or paint applied to a canvas before painting.

GUILD An independent association of artisans, bankers, or manufacturers who were responsible for recruitment and for maintaining levels of workmanship.

HUMANISM Cultural movement of the Renaissance in which prime importance was given to human reason rather than to God's word and revelation.

LAST SUPPER The last meal that Christ took with his 12 disciples before his arrest, when he told them that one of them would betray him.

MAJOLICA Pottery decorated in bright colours over a glazed white background, first imported into Italy from Spain around 1450.

MASTERPIECE An artist's most outstanding piece of work, or one done with extraordinary skill. This is also known as a masterwork, from the piece of work presented to a medieval guild showing whether an apprentice had the skill to become a master at his craft. (*see also* APPRENTICE)

MEDIUM In painting, the substance that binds the pigment – for example, in oil paint the medium is an oil (such as poppy oil); in tempera the medium is egg. (*see also* OIL PAINTING, PIGMENT, TEMPERA)

MIDDLE GROUND Area between the foreground and the background of a painting.

MORTAR Bowl made of wood or stone which is used with a pestle to grind pigment into powder. (*see also* PESTLE, PIGMENT)

MURAL Large design usually created on the wall of a public building, often using the technique of fresco. (*see also* FRESCO)

OIL PAINTING A technique in which powdered pigment is mixed with a medium of slow-drying oil, such as linseed, walnut, or poppy. The oil absorbs oxygen from the air and forms a transparent skin that locks in the colour.

PALETTE Small square slab of wood, stone, or ivory on which painters laid out their colours, first used in the 1400s. Palettes were made larger and kidney-shaped in the 1800s, with a hole for the artist's thumb.

PANEL A hard surface, usually wood, which may be painted. Renaissance artists often painted on panels with tempera or oil paints. The panels were prepared beforehand with a layer of gesso. (*see also* GESSO, TEMPERA)

PATRON Person who commissions and pays for a work of art.

PERSPECTIVE A way of drawing three-dimensional objects on a flat, two-dimensional surface, to create a sense of depth, or receding space. (*see also* FORESHORTENING, PICTURE PLANE)

PESTLE A tool made of hard wood or stone which is used to crush or grind pigments into powder in a bowl called a mortar. (*see also* MORTAR, PIGMENT)

PICTURE PLANE The flat surface on which a picture is painted. The vertical plane is imagined as a window pane between the viewer (or artist) and the scene in the picture.

Blue pigment

PIGMENT Coloured powder, used in making paint, taken from a plant, animal, or mineral. For example, ultramarine blue came from ground lapis lazuli or azurite, and crimson from crushed cochineal beetles.

PLANE Any flat or level surface.

PREDELLA PANEL A row of small paintings set below the main panel of an altarpiece. The panel often contains scenes from the lives of the saints represented above. (*see also* ALTARPIECE)

PRIMARY COLOURS The three colours (red, blue, and yellow) from which all other colours are derived.

REFORMATION Religious and political movement of 16th-century Europe that began as an attempt to reform the Roman Catholic Church and resulted in the formation of Protestant Churches.

RELIEF From the Italian word for "raised", a type of sculpture that projects from a back panel, which is itself part of the sculpture.

RENAISSANCE The great revival of art, literature, and learning in Europe during the 14th, 15th, and 16th centuries.

SCULPTURE Three-dimensional work of art that can be carved, modelled, built, or cast. (*see also* RELIEF)

SINOPIA A technique that uses red ochre to draw initial guides for fresco painting.

SIZE A clear glue made by boiling animal skins, and used to prime or coat bare wood before it was painted with gesso (*see also* GESSO)

SFUMATO A technique (especially applied to the work of Leonardo) in which the blending of oil paint and outlines makes forms merge into one another. The term is derived from the Italian word *fumo*, meaning "smoke".

TEMPERA A technique in which pigment is dissolved in water and mixed with gum or egg yolk rather than oil. (*see also* EGG TEMPERA)

Tondo showing *Madonna and Child* by Fra Filippo Lippi

TONDO A circular painting.

TONE Lightness or darkness of a colour on a scale from black to white.

TRIPTYCH A painting made up of three panels, usually hinged so that the side panels can be folded towards the centre panel; a common form of altarpiece during the Renaissance.

UNIVERSAL MAN Phrase coined in 1860 by Jacob Burckhardt, an historian of the Renaissance, to describe Leonardo.

VANISHING POINT The single point in a painting where all parallel lines – from the viewer to the horizon line – appear to meet. The vanishing point in a painting is usually placed at the eye level of the viewer. (*see also* PERSPECTIVE)

WORKSHOP The artist's studio and the apprentices and trained artists who worked there with a master. (*see also* APPRENTICE)

Relief by sculptor Luca della Robbia for Florence Cathedral

Index

Acknowledgements

Dorling Kindersley would like to thank: Alan Hills and Dora Thornton at the British Museum; the Museum of London; the Shakespeare Globe Trust; Signora Pelliconi at the Soprintendenza per i beni artistici e strorici; the Museo Horne; the Bargello in Florence (photographs used on concession by the Ministry of Beni Culturali ed Ambientali, Florence).

Art consultants: Alison Cole, Jill Dunkerton

Map: John Woodcock

Modelmaker: Peter Griffiths

Additional photography: Gary Ombler

Index: Chris Bernstein

In-house assistance: Robert Graham, Bethany Dawn, Jill Bunyan, Anna Martin, Rose Hardy

The publisher would like to thank the following for their kind permission to reproduce their photographs:

Key: a=above; b=below; c=centre; l=left; r=right; t=top

Abbreviations:
AKG: AKG London; BAL: Bridgeman Art Library, London; MEPL: Mary Evans Picture Library; SCA: Scala Firenze; V&A: Victoria and Albert Museum, London.

Page 9 bl Bibliotheque Nationale, Paris/AKG; tr Cott Nero E II pt2 f.20v *The Expulsion of the Albigensians from Carcassonne: Catherist heretics of the 12th and 13th centuries*, from "The Chronicles of France, from Priam King of Troy until the crowning of Charles VI", (by the Boucicaut Master and Workshop, Chronicles of France, 1388 British Library, London)/BAL; br MEPL;

Pages 10-11 p10: bl Frontispiece to Petrarch's Copy of Maurius Servius Honoratus's "Commentary on Virgil", 1340 by Simone Martini (1284-1344) Biblioteca Ambrosiana, Milan/BAL; tl Museo Pio-Clementino Vaticano/ SCA; p11: tr, detail *Primavera*, c.1478, (tempera on panel) by Sandro Botticelli (1444/5-1510) Galleria Degli Uffizi, Firenze/BAL; tl Museo dell' Opera Metropolitana, Siena/SCA; br Palazzo Vecchio, Firenze/SCA;

Pages 12-13 p12: br, detail *Portrait of Lionello d'Este* by Antonio Pisanello (1395-1455) Galleria dell'Accademia Carrara, Bergamo/BAL; tl SCA; bl, detail Pinacoteca di Brera Milano/SCA; p13: bl, detail Federigo da Montefeltro, Duke of Urbino, c.1465 (panel) by Piero della Francesca (c.1419/21-92) Galleria Degli Uffizi, Firenze/BAL; tr Museo Dell' Opera del Duomo, Firenze/SCA;

Pages 14-15 p14: r, detail *Portrait of Henry VIII* by Hans the Younger Holbein (1497/8-1543) Belvoir Castle, Leicestershire, UK/BAL; p15: l, detail AKG; r, detail Vatican Museum, Rome/AKG; tc *Portrait of Francis I on Horseback*, c.1540 by Francois Clouet (c.1510-72) Galleria degli Uffizi, Firenze/BAL; tr Accademia Venezia/SCA;

Pages 16-17 p16: bl National Maritime Museum; br MEPL; tr MEPL; p17: tl British Museum;

Pages 18-19 p18: tl *Equestrian Monument of Sir John Hawkwood* (fresco) by Paolo Uccello (1397-1475) Duomo, Firenze/BAL; c *Henry VIII (1491-1547)* and *Parliament in 1523* (engraving) by English School (16th century) Private Collection/BAL; p19: tr Museo di San Marco, Firenze/AKG; tl *Portrait of Niccolo Machiavelli* (1469-1527) by Santi di Tito (1536-1603) Palazzo Vecchio, Firenze/BAL; c MEPL.

Pages 20-21 p20: l SCA; br SCA; p21: b, detail *Adoration of the Magi* by Sandro Botticelli (1444/5-1510) Galleria Degli Uffizi, Firenze /BAL; tl *Portrait Bust of Lorenzo de' Medici* by Andrea del Verrocchio (1435-88) Palazzo Medici-Riccardi, Firenze/BAL; tc SC.

Pages 22-23 p22: bc AKG; br, detail *Libyan Sibyl* by Michelangelo Buonarroti (1475-1564) Vatican Museums and Galleries, Rome/BAL; c Louvre, Paris/ET Archive.

Pages 26-27 p26: br *The Lady with the Ermine* (Cecilia Gallerani) by Leonardo da Vinci (1452-1519) Czartorisky Museum, Krakow/BAL; p27: tr Ginevra deí Benci (Reverse) © 1999 Board of Trustees, National Gallery of Art, Washington; br V&A.

Pages 28-29 p28: tl View of the main altar (photo) San Miniato Al Monte, Firenze/BAL; br National Gallery, London; bl National Gallery, London; p29: br Fr 12420 f.86 *The Story of Thamyris*, from 'De Claris Mulieribus' "Works of Giovanni Boccaccio" (1313-75) Bibliotheque Nationale, Paris/BAL; tl National Gallery, London; cb gemstones Natural History Museum.

Pages 30-31 p30: tl detail Fort Belvedere and the Pitti Palace from a series of lunettes depicting views of the Medici Villas, 1599 by Giusto Utens (fl.1599-1609) Museo di Firenze Com'era, Firenze/BAL; c Corbis UK Ltd; cl Royal Collection Enterprises (The Royal Collection ©1999 Her Majesty Queen Elizabeth II); 30-31 b SCA; p31: tl The Month of October, c.1400 (fresco) by Italian School (15th Century) Castello del Buonconsiglio, Trent/BAL; tr Royal Collection Enterprises (The Royal Collection ©1999 Her Majesty Queen Elizabeth II); cr Royal Collection Enterprises (The Royal Collection ©1999 Her Majesty Queen Elizabeth II);

Pages 32-33 p32: bc Warburg Institute (University of London); p33: br AKG;

Pages 34-35 p34: tl Szepmueveszeti Muzeum, Budapest AKG; cl *Study for the Battle of Anghiari*, 1504-5 (pen & ink) by Leonardo da Vinci (1452-1519) Galleria dell' Accademia, Venice/BAL; bl Daspet; cr Mus. du Louvre, Paris/Photographie Giraudon; p35: cl Museo Nazionale del Bargello, Firenze/AKG; tr *Figure Study for Battle of Cascina* 1504, pen, brush, brown and grey ink (W.6 recto) by Michelangelo Buonarroti (1475-1564) British Museum, London/BAL; tl *The Battle of Cascina*, after Michelangelo (1475-1564) by Antonio da Sangallo, the elder (1455-1534) Holkham Hall, Norfolk/BAL; clb *The Sacrifice of Isaac*, bronze competition relief for the Baptistry Doors, Firenze, 1401-2 by Filippo Brunelleschi (1377-1446) Museo Nazionale del Bargello, Firenze/BAL;

Pages 36-37 p36: tl, detail *Warrior with Groom (II Gattamelata)* by Giorgione (Giorgio da Castelfranco) (1476/8-1510) Galleria Degli Ufffizi, Firenze/BAL; bl, detail British Museum, London; p37: tl Musee du Louvre; bl *Portrait of a Child* by Sofonisba Anguiscola (1527-1625) ; The Trustees of Weston Park Foundation/BAL; r, detail *Portrait of Dona Margarita de Cardona, wife of Count Adam of Dietrichstein* (oil on canvas) by Titian follower Roudnice Lobkowicz Coll., Nelahozeves Castle, Czech Republic /BAL;

Pages 38-39 p38: bl Vinci Tourist Office; p39: crb V&A;

Pages 42-43 p42: bc Image Select; bl, detail Oeffentliche Kunstsammlung Basel, Kunstmuseum; r The Wellcome Trust (Wellcome Institute Library, London); p43: tl Hunter 364 (TOP V14 f.59) *John Bannister delivering an anatomy lesson* Glasgow Universiry Library/BAL; bc Royal Collection Enterprises (The Royal Collection ©1999 Her Majesty Queen Elizabeth II); br Royal Collection Enterprises (The Royal Collection ©1999 Her Majesty Queen Elizabeth II), bl Science Museum;

Pages 44-45 p44: c Hulton Getty; bl Museo della Scienza e della Tecnica, Milano/SCA; 44-45 t Museo della Scienza e della Tecnica, Milano/SCA; p45: br MEPL;

Pages 46-47 p46: cr MEPL (Explorer Archives); tl Hulton Getty; bl, detail SCA; br Science Photo Library; p47: tl MEPL; tr Hulton Getty; bl Biblioteca Nazionale, Firenze/SCA; c Museo della Scienza, Firenze/SCA; cl Science Photo Library;

Pages 48-49 p48: b Museo Nazionale della Scienza e della Tecnica "Leonardo da Vinci"; ac Science & Society Picture Library; cr Science & Society Picture Library; p49: c, detail *Head of a Warrior* (drawing) by Leonardo da Vinci (1452-1519) British Museum, London/BAL; bl and ac Wallace Collection, London;

Pages 50-51 p50: cra Biblioteca Laurenziana, Firenze/SCA; bc Museum of London; tc both Science Museum, London p51: tr MEPL;

Pages 52-53 p52: l Add 42130 f.182v Text, and grotesque - the hybrid monster composed of animal and human parts, begun prior to 1340 for Sir Geoffrey Luttrell (1276-1345), Latin, Luttrell Psalter, (14th century) British Library, London/BAL; c British Library; br MEPL; tr MEPL; p53: t Add 42130 f.182v Text, and grotesque - the hybrid monster composed of animal and human parts, begun prior to 1340 for Sir Geoffrey Luttrell (1276-1345), Latin, Luttrell Psalter, (14th century) British Library, London/BAL; c St Bride Printing Library;

Pages 54-55 p54: tl MEPL; Kunsthistorisches Museum ; cl Lebrecht Collection; bl, detail SCA; p55: cr, detail AKG; br *The Stock Market*;

Pages 56-57 p58: cl *Adam* by Albrecht Durer (1471-1528) Prado, Madrid/BAL; br *Charon Crossing the River Styx* by Joachim Patenier or Patinir (1487-1524) Prado, Madrid/BAL; c *Eve* by Albrecht Durer (1471-1528) Prado, Madrid/BAL; cr *Hunters in the Snow - February 1565* by Pieter Brueghel the Elder (c.1515-69) Kunsthistorisches Museum, Vienna/BAL; tc MEPL; p59: tr AKG; bl National Gallery, London/AKG; tl *Portrait of Deiderius Erasmus* (1466-1536) (oil on panel) by Hans the Younger Holbein (1497/8-1543) Louvre, Paris/BAL; cr MEPL; br National Trust Photographic Library.

Pages 58-59 p56: tc, detail *Self Portrait, 1629* by Harmensz van Rijn Rembrandt (1606-69) Mauritshuis, The Hague, Netherlands/BAL; cra, detail *Self Portrait, 1661-62* by Harmensz van Rijn Rembrandt (1606-69) Kenwood House, London/BAL; bl MEPL; c Tony Stone Images (John Lawrence); p57: tl *François I Cradling the Dying Leonardo da Vinci*, 1818 by Jean Auguste Dominique Ingres (1780-1867) Musee du Petit Palais, Paris/BAL; tr Science Museum.

Pages 60-61 background Private Collection/BAL; p60: tl Courtesy of The British Library; br © EMPICS Ltd; bl SCA; p61: tl Courtesy of the Musée du Louvre, Paris

Pages 62-63 p62: l SCA; p63: t SCA;

Pages 64-65 background Erich Lessing/AKG; p64: tl Private Collection, Boltin Picture Library/BAL; tr B.S.P.I/CORBIS; cl Erich Lessing/AKG; p65: tl V&A Images/Victoria and Albert Museum; ca Sandro Vannini/CORBIS; br Hermitage, St Petersburg, Russia/www.bridgeman.co.uk

Pages 66-67 p67: cr Rabatti – Dominige/AKG

Pages 68-69 Santa Maria della Grazie, Milan, Italy/BAL

All other images © Dorling Kindersley
For further information see:
www.dkimages.com

Eyewitness titles in this series: